MEDIEVAL WORLD

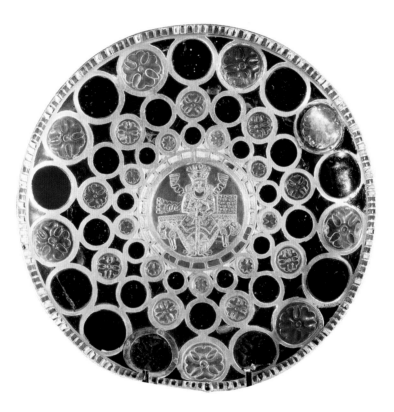

Volume 9

ROME — THOMAS AQUINAS

GROLIER

Published by Grolier Educational
Sherman Turnpike
Danbury, Connecticut 06816

© 2001 The Brown Reference Group plc
Reprinted in 2003

Set ISBN 0-7172-5520-4 (set)
Volume ISBN 0-7172-5529-8

Library of Congress Cataloging-in-Publication Data
Medieval world
　　　p.cm.
　　Includes bibliographical references and index.
　　Contents: v.1. Abelard–Burgundy—v.2. Byzantine
Empire–Constantinople—v.3. Copts–Feudalism—v.4.
Florence–Hospitals—v.5. House and home–Joan of
Arc—v.6. Justinian–Mediterranean—v.7. Mehmed II–
Painting and sculpture—v.8. Papacy–Roman Empire—
v.9. Rome–Thomas Aquinas—v.10. Tools and
technology–Writing.
　　ISBN 0-7172-5520-4 (set)—ISBN 0-7172-5521-2
(v.1)—ISBN 0-7172-5522-0 (v.2)—ISBN 0-7172-
5523-9 (v.3)—ISBN 0-7172-5524-7 (v.4)—ISBN
0-7172-5525-5 (v.5)—ISBN 0-7172-5526-3 (v.6)—
ISBN 0-7172-5527-1 (v.7)—ISBN 0-7172-5528-X
(v.8)—ISBN 0-7172-5529-8 (v.9)—ISBN 0-7172-
5530-1 (v.10)
　　　1. Middle Ages—Juvenile literature. 2. Civilization,
　　Medieval—Juvenile literature. I.
　　Grolier Educational (Firm)

　　D117.D37 2001
　　909'.1—dc21　　　　　　　　00-046649

For information address the publisher:
Grolier Educational, Sherman Turnpike,
Danbury, Connecticut 06816

FOR THE BROWN REFERENCE GROUP PLC
Project Editor:　　　　　Sally MacEachern
Designer:　　　　　　　Sarah Williams
Picture Researcher:　　　Veneta Bullen
Text Editors:　　　　　　Rachel Bean, Chris King,
　　　　　　　　　　　　Sally MacEachern
Maps:　　　　　　　　　Mark Walker
Indexer:　　　　　　　　Kay Ollerenshaw
Design Manager:　　　　Lynne Ross
Production Manager:　　　Matt Weyland
Managing Editor:　　　　Tim Cooke
Consultant:　　　　　　　Fredric L. Cheyette
　　　　　　　　　　　　Amherst College MA

Printed and bound in Singapore

ABOUT THIS BOOK

◆

This set of 10 books tells the stories of the individuals, peoples, battles, treaties, empires, ideas, and religions that shaped the period we call the Middle Ages. When did the Middle Ages begin and end? Historians often suggest that they began in 476, when the last western Roman emperor was deposed by a barbarian chief, and that they ended in 1453, when the Ottoman Turks captured Constantinople, the capital of the eastern Roman empire. These dates, however, are only convenient markers. The Middle Ages were both a continuation of what had gone before, as well as a time of immense social and political change, while advances in architecture, art, literature, and learning paved the way for the period called the Renaissance that began in the 15th century.

The set focuses on Europe, but it also shows how other civilizations such as China, India, and Africa were developing, and the ways in which the Islamic and Christian worlds interacted on many different levels.

The entries in this set are arranged alphabetically and are illustrated with photographs, drawings, and maps. Many of the illustrations come from medieval sources. Each entry ends with a list of cross-references to other entries in the set. They will enable you to find entries on closely related subjects that will help expand and build on your knowledge. At the end of each book there is a timeline to help you relate events to one another in time. There is also a useful "Further Reading" list that includes websites, a glossary of special terms, and an index covering the whole set.

MAPS

The maps in this book show the locations of cities, states, and empires in the Middle Ages. However, for the sake of clarity and ease of use, modern place names are often used.

CONTENTS

VOLUME 9

ROME

As the capital of a vast empire, ancient Rome had been a grand and powerful city, but by the Middle Ages it was in decline. With the collapse of the Roman Empire, barbarian invasions, and outbreaks of the plague, its population shrank, and its great buildings fell into ruin. Yet despite its changing fortunes, the city remained important as the home of the pope and the Roman Catholic church.

I n its heyday Rome was the capital of an empire that stretched from North Africa in the south to Scotland in the north, and from Spain in the west to Syria in the east. It was a flourishing and powerful city with a population of over one million at the turn of the first and second centuries A.D. Its administrative heart was a complex of grand buildings called the Forum, and palaces, gardens, temples, theaters, markets, public spaces, and stadiums filled the city.

DECLINE AND RUIN

However, from the end of the second century the city began a long process of decline that was only halted in the 16th century. Political and economic problems beset the empire, and a plague epidemic wiped out a large part of Rome's population. From 408 Rome was also subject to repeated barbarian attacks: It was sacked in 410 by the Visigoths and in 455 by the Vandals. In 476 the last emperor, Romulus Augustus, was deposed by the Ostrogoth ruler Theodoric.

By 500 the aqueducts that supplied Rome with water had been destroyed both by invaders and by Roman citizens, who took the lead from the pipes to use in their buildings. The great monuments had also fallen into ruin; some were converted to other uses, and many were pillaged for building materials. Blocks of cut stone and bricks were taken to put up new buildings, and marble was burned to make lime (used to make cement.)

With limited water supplies the population moved down from the seven hills of Rome, where the fashionable residences had once stood, and became concentrated around the Tiber River that flowed through the city. Much of the area enclosed by the city walls reverted to marsh and pasture, and the city's population dropped to around 30,000 for most of the Middle Ages.

Although Rome had lost its former power and wealth, it nonetheless derived a new authority from being the home of the pope and the Roman Catholic church. Foreign rulers—

A view of Rome from a 15th-century fresco, or wall painting, showing the medieval city inside its ancient city walls. At left are the ruins of the Forum and Colosseum; in the center buildings cluster around the Tiber River; and the Vatican stands on the far side of the river.

HOME OF THE POPES

The first papal residence in Rome was the Lateran Palace, which stood next to the Basilica of San Giovanni in the southeast of the city. San Giovanni is Rome's cathedral and was founded by Emperor Constantine in the fourth century. However, after Muslims plundered the church of St. Peter's in 846, Pope Leo IV built a strong defensive wall around the neighborhood in which it stood: the Vatican. Popes took refuge there in times of unrest, and it became their permanent home when they returned from Avignon at the end of the 14th century. They embarked on a large construction program that included rebuilding St. Peter's, the most important Roman Catholic church.

including the Byzantine emperors and Frankish kings—and powerful Roman families continually sought to dominate and influence the pope. The resulting power struggles brought constant instability to Rome during the Middle Ages.

Despite this instability, by the 11th century the popes had made the city a center of pilgrimage. Because there was little in the way of manufacturing or industry in Rome, the money pilgrims spent on food, lodgings, and gifts to the church was a vital part of the city's economy.

However, as a result of political rivalry between the French kings and powerful Roman families, the power of the pope was severely weakened in the 14th century. The papacy was forced to leave Rome altogether between 1309 and 1377, and two rival popes were elected during a period known as the Great Schism (1378–1417). Around 1400 Rome was described as a city filled with huts, thieves, and vermin.

It was not until the rule of powerful popes in the 15th and 16th centuries that the papacy and the city became strong and stable again. The government was reformed, the squalid medieval streets were cleaned up, and new buildings were commissioned as Rome became a center of the great artistic revival, or Renaissance.

View of the Forum with the Temple of Castor and Pollux and Hadrian's Basilica, **painted in 1600 by the Dutch painter Paul Brill. The scene was similar in the Middle Ages, when the Forum became known as the Campo Vaccino, which means "cow field."**

RUSSIA

During the early Middle Ages the western part of the vast region that is now Russia was occupied by Slavic farming people. The eastern part was home to nomadic tribes. As Vikings arrived, city-states grew in the west, and the most important of them developed around Kiev. After a Mongol invasion in the 13th century the Moscow region quickly grew in power and influence.

In the ninth century Swedish Vikings, whom the Slavs called Varangians, made their way down the Dnieper, Volga, and other rivers, establishing trading towns as they went. In 862 a group of Varangian families moved to the northern settlement of Novgorod, where they lived under their leader Rurik. Some medieval sources say that the local Slavs invited the newcomers to rule over them because they wanted to bring order to their society.

KIEVAN RUS

In 882 Rurik's successor, Oleg, made the town of Kiev his capital. It eventually became the center of a region historians now call Kievan Rus. People are divided as to where the name Rus actually came from. Some scholars believe it developed from *Ruotsi*, a Finnish word for the Swedes or Varangians,

while others think it might have been the name of a Slavic tribe from the Black Sea region.

Whatever the exact origins of the name, Kievan Rus quickly became an important state, populated by both Slavs and Varangians. It traded extensively with the Byzantine Empire to the south. The state was pagan until the 10th century. Then Vladimir I, the grand prince of Kiev, adopted the Byzantine religion of Christianity, forcing his subjects to give up their old gods and become Christians as well. This act helped give the state of Kiev a sense of unity.

This 15th-century painting shows scenes from a battle between the cities of Suzdal and Novgorod in 1169. In the top panel the citizens of Novgorod are praying to an icon to bring them victory in the battle.

Kiev flourished for most of the 11th century, but then declined. One reason for this was that northern cities became increasingly independent, developing closer ties with the cities of the Baltic and northern Europe. In 1169 Andrew Bogolyubsky of the city of Suzdal attacked and took Kiev. Although he claimed the title of grand prince of Kiev, he destroyed much of the city and made Vladimir the new capital of Kievan Rus.

MONGOL INVASIONS

Early in the 13th century a great threat to all the Russian principalities came sweeping in from the east. Under the leadership of Batu, the grandson of Genghis Khan, Mongol horsemen crossed the frozen Volga River in 1237. After a five-day siege the Mongols—called Tartars by the Russians—destroyed the town of Ryazan. Vladimir followed, before the invaders turned south and destroyed

NOVGOROD

Novgorod, situated on the Volkhov River in northwestern Russia, was founded as a trading settlement in the ninth century. The town grew rapidly and in 1019 started to govern itself. The town assembly, or *veche*, elected successive princes, who acted chiefly as military commanders. The town was divided into five "ends," each with its own administrative assembly.

Novgorod was strategically situated on the trade network that linked the Baltic Sea in the north and the Black Sea in the south. It was a hub of mercantile activity, its craftworkers and traders supplying a wide range of goods—jewelry, leather, glass, and pottery—to merchants from Scandinavia and northern Germany. The main local exports were wax (much in demand for the candles in Europe's churches) and furs, while a wide range of products, including wine, incense, spices, timber, and cloth, passed through the town. Because of its location Novgorod escaped Mongol invasion in the 13th century, but was involved in a long struggle for supremacy with the rising city of Moscow in the 14th and 15th centuries.

The Kremlin of Novgorod. The city's first stone kremlin, or fortified enclosure, was built in 1420.

Kiev in 1240. Batu set up his capital at Sarai near the Caspian Sea. He allowed Russian princes to keep their local power so long as they paid tribute and homage to him at Sarai.

At the time of the Mongol invasion the prince of Novgorod was Alexander Nevsky (about 1220–1263). Despite opposition from many of his people, Alexander decided it was best to pay tribute to the Mongols rather than have his principality destroyed.

One reason why Alexander was so willing to accommodate the Mongols was that Novgorod faced dangers from the west as well. In 1240 Alexander defeated a Swedish army at a battle near the Neva River, and it was in honor of this victory that the title Nevsky was added to his name. Two years later he defeated the Teutonic Knights in the Battle on the Ice at Lake Peipus.

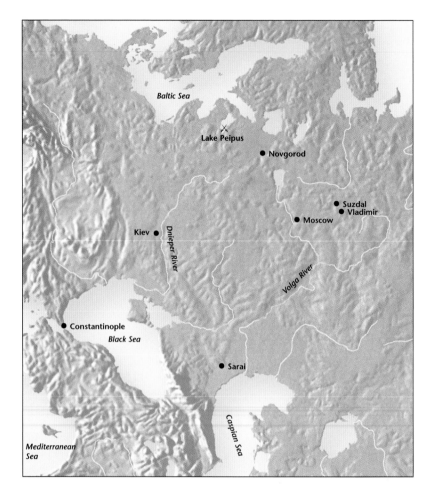

This map of medieval Russia shows its most important cities.

RISE OF MOSCOW

During the reign of Alexander Nevsky Moscow was a relatively unimportant town, but over the following century it grew rapidly in size. Alexander Nevsky's youngest son Daniel (1261–1303) became prince of Moscow in 1276. Daniel spent much of his reign trying to build up his tiny principality, expanding its territory along the banks of the Moscow River.

However, it was under the reign of Daniel's son, Ivan I (ruled 1328–1341), that Moscow really expanded. Ivan collected taxes on behalf of the

THE BATTLE ON THE ICE

One of the most famous victories of Alexander Nevsky was the Battle on the Ice, where he defeated the forces of the Teutonic Knights. The knights had begun to attack northwest Russia in 1239, capturing the city of Pskov in 1241. Alexander quickly launched a counteroffensive, retaking the city and driving the knights back into Estonia. He delivered a decisive blow at Lake Peipus, or Chud, in 1242.

The heavy cavalry of the Teutonic Knights made a brutal frontal assault on the Russian army. However, Alexander managed to outmaneuver his opponents, attacking their flanks and drawing them onto the frozen lake. There the weight of the knights' armor cracked the thin spring ice. Thousands drowned, and the Teutonic Knights were routed. Alexander's victory is one of the most celebrated events in Russian history.

Mongols, and he took advantage of the position to build up a personal fortune. Ivan used this money to increase the territory of Muscovy, the land around Moscow. Other Russian princes and nobles began to serve Moscow as it became the leading city in the area.

During Ivan's reign Moscow also became the center of Russian orthodoxy. In 1326 the head of the Russian church died while visiting Moscow. He was later canonized as Saint Peter, and the city became a place of pilgrimage. Two years later Ivan persuaded Peter's successor, Theognost, to relocate from Vladimir to Moscow. The move greatly added to the city's prestige

MONGOL DECLINE

Toward the end of the 14th century the power of the Mongols began to decline. After the death of the Mongol leader Jani Beg in 1357 the Mongol tribes increasingly fought among themselves. In 1380 Dmitry II (1350–1389), the grand prince of Moscow, defeated a Mongol force at the Battle of Kulikovo, near the Don River. His victory earned him the nickname Dmitry Donskoy, or "Dmitry of the Don." The Mongols avenged the defeat two years later, but the balance of power was changing.

The rise of Moscow continued in the 15th century. Grand Prince Ivan III, known as "the Great" (1440–1505), expanded the territory of Muscovy even further. Ivan came to power in 1462 and gradually began to bring rival towns and cities under his control. The most important was Novgorod, which fell to Muscovite forces in 1478.

In 1480 Ivan finally stopped the payment of taxes to the Mongols. A Mongol attempt to reassert their authority came to nothing, and by the end of Ivan's reign Muscovy was a powerful, independent state, the forerunner of modern Russia.

The Ivan the Great Bell Tower, built between 1505 and 1508, stands at the heart of Moscow's Kremlin.

SEE ALSO

- Hanseatic League
- Kiev
- Mongols
- Orthodox Church
- Slavic Peoples
- Vikings

SALADIN

Saladin (about 1138–1193), sultan of Syria and Egypt, was a great Muslim general who fought against the Christians during the Crusades. In 1187 Saladin defeated a large army of Crusaders and captured the holy city of Jerusalem in Palestine.

Salah ad–Din Yusuf ibn Ayyub, or Saladin, was born in Tikrit in modern Iraq. He came from a Turkic military family. The Turks had provided the backbone of Muslim armies for over two centuries, and Saladin's uncle, Shirkuh, was a general in the army of the Syrian Muslim leader Nur ad-Din Zengi. At a young age Saladin became a soldier too. In 1164 he joined his uncle's army on campaign in Egypt, where the Syrians were fighting both the Crusaders and a rival Muslim sect. When the Syrians took control of Egypt, Saladin was made the country's vizier, in charge of the government. Later he became Egypt's sultan, or supreme ruler.

Nur ad-Din died in 1174. Now Saladin decided to take over his kingdom too. It took him over 10 years to work his way northward, capturing the Syrian cities of Damascus, Aleppo, and Edessa. By the late 1180s he had united the kingdoms of Syria and Egypt.

HOLY WAR

Now Saladin turned his attention to the *jihad*, or holy war, against the Crusaders, who in the 11th century had established a Christian kingdom in Palestine. Its capital was the holy city of Jerusalem. In 1187 Saladin destroyed a large army of Crusaders at the Battle of Hattin. Later that year he conquered Jerusalem itself.

A 16th-century Italian painting of the Muslim general Saladin. Saladin was one of the greatest military leaders of the Middle Ages.

In 1189 the Christians launched a new Crusade to try to recapture Jerusalem. Saladin withstood their attacks and later made a treaty with the Crusader leader Richard the Lionheart. The treaty allowed Christian pilgrims to visit Jerusalem.

Saladin died of yellow fever in March 1193. He was remembered not only as a great general, but also as a fair and thoughtful leader who showed tolerance and restraint in his dealings with the peoples he conquered. Most importantly, he brought a unity and strength of purpose to the Islamic world that allowed it to withstand the assaults of the Christian Crusaders.

SEE ALSO

♦ Crusader States
♦ Crusades
♦ Islam
♦ Islamic Empire
♦ Jerusalem

SASSANID EMPIRE

The Sassanid, or Sassanian, Empire was based on Persia (modern Iran). The Sassanid dynasty ruled from 224 to 651. It was named after Sasan, the grandfather of the first ruler, Ardashir I (ruled 224–241).

The Sassanids ruled fro[...] capital of Ctesiphon, [...] Tigris River in moder[...] The empire was frequently at [...] with the Roman Empire, the Byzantine Empire, and a serie[...] nomadic invaders from Centr[...] Asia, India, and Afghanistan. Despite this, art flourished, and the Sassanid rulers built cities and roads, as well as improving and extending the irrigation system.

Conserving water was vital in a region that never had much rainfall. Since ancient times the Persians ha[...] built underground water channels called *ghanats*. They sank a well down to a water source on sloping ground, an[...] they dug horizontal channels that allowed water to flow to [...] surface. It was difficult, dang[...] work, but the results were hi[...] effective. The method is still [...] some parts of Iran, where there are more than 50,000 *ghanats*.

HEIGHT OF POWER

The Sassanid Empire reached its height in the sixth century. One of its greatest kings was Khosrow I (ruled 531–579), who was known to the Persians as Khosrow of the Immortal Soul. Khosrow reduced the power previously enjoyed by regional

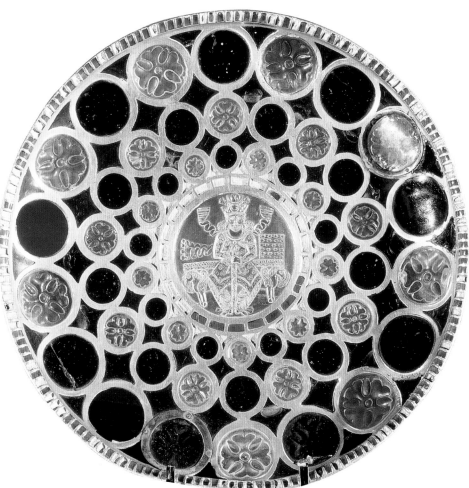

This dish is made from gold, rock crystal, and polished granite. In the center is an image of Khosrow I on his throne.

lords, introduced a fairer taxation system, and reorganized the administration of the empire. He appointed four commanders to guard the four borders of his empire, and his army conquered Antioch (in modern Turkey) and marched southwest as far as Yemen on the Arabian Peninsula, which became a Sassanid dependency. He also built many palaces, roads, and bridges.

ROCK SCULPTURE

The Sassanid period is famous for its great rock sculptures. More than 30 still exist in various parts of Iran. They generally depict victories in battle, gods, and the crowning of kings. They were carved in high relief, which means that the figures were part of the rock face but had a three-dimensional quality. The cliffs are limestone, which is soft and relatively easy to carve. The kings can usually be identified by their crowns, which were different for each ruler.

This limestone cliff carving shows Shapur I (died 272) capturing the Roman emperor Valerian. This scene was a favorite subject for Sassanid artists. Valerian remained Shapur's prisoner until he died.

Khosrow's court was renowned for its learning. Medicine and astronomy flourished, and the legends of ancient Persia were revived and recorded. Some scholars believe that Khosrow had a special alphabet created to record the sacred texts of the Zoroastrian religion. In 529, when the ancient academy of Athens was closed, a number of Greek philosophers, or thinkers, moved to Ctesiphon. It is said that Khosrow also brought the game of chess to Persia from India.

SASSANID DECLINE

The last great Sassanid ruler, Khosrow II (ruled 590–628), sent his armies into Anatolia, Syria, and Egypt. In 614 they sacked Jerusalem and took away the relic of the True Cross, the city's most valued treasure. Khosrow II was an enthusiastic patron of the arts. Silverworking and carpetmaking reached a peak during his reign.

Between 622 and 627, however, the Byzantine army led by Emperor Heraclius (ruled 610–641) reversed the Persian wave of conquests. In 628 Khosrow was killed by his own son. After his death the Sassanids declined. In 637 they suffered a crushing defeat at the hands of Arabs, who were moving northeastward from the Arabian Peninsula. The Arabs were the warriors of a new religion called Islam, founded by the prophet Muhammad, who had died five years earlier. Sassanid Persia became the first of many Arab conquests. The last ruler of the Sassanid dynasty was killed in 651.

SEE ALSO

♦ Arabs
♦ Byzantine Empire
♦ Islam
♦ Islamic Empire
♦ Persia
♦ Relics

SCANDINAVIA

Scandinavia is made up of the northern European countries of Denmark, Norway, and Sweden. During the Middle Ages these countries formed the homelands of the seafaring Vikings. Scandinavia was originally inhabited by independent tribes. However, by the end of the 14th century it was united under a single ruler.

I n the early Middle Ages the people of Scandinavia lived in small settlements governed by local chieftains. The people who lived in these villages were farmers who grew cereals such as barley and oats and vegetables such as beans and cabbage. They also reared cattle, pigs, and sheep, while those on the coast fished and traded. The Scandinavians had a distinctive culture. They worshiped their own pagan gods, such as Odin and Thor, and had their own mythology, based on tales of great Norse heroes that were handed down through the generations.

EARLY KINGDOMS

During the seventh century the most powerful Scandinavian chieftains began to extend their control over regional kingdoms. One of the earliest of these kingdoms was based on the peninsula of Jutland, which today forms the continental part of Denmark (the rest of the country is made up of islands) and the northern tip of Germany. In 737 the Danes who lived in Jutland built an earthwork rampart, called the Dannevirke, all across the peninsula from the Baltic to the North Sea. Their king, Angantyr, put up this defensive barrier in order to stop the Franks from moving northward and invading his territory.

The Jelling Stones, erected in the 10th century in Denmark in memory of the parents of Harold I Bluetooth.

From the end of the eighth century onward groups of adventurers from all over Scandinavia began to launch attacks on the rest of Europe. They became known as Vikings, from the Norse word for "seafarer." In the west marauding bands from Norway and Denmark conducted a series of

This map shows the Viking homelands of Sweden, Norway, and Denmark. From these lands the Vikings launched raids on much of northern Europe.

devastating raids on coastal settlements in the British Isles and northern France. Eventually, they began to settle in these areas. In the east seafarers from Sweden traveled down rivers toward the Black and Caspian Seas, establishing trading settlements along the way. Historians are unsure why these migrations happened. Some believe that a growth in population forced the Vikings to seek new land, others that the opportunities for plunder were simply too good to ignore.

Another theory as to why so many Vikings left their homes was that they were driven away after internal struggles between rival leaders. For most of the early Middle Ages Scandinavia was made up of a patchwork of tiny kingdoms, and they were often at war with one another. Gradually, however, large unified kingdoms began to emerge. In 890 Harald Finehair (died 940) managed to unite the various tribal clans of Norway. In the middle of the 10th century the whole of Denmark came under the control of Harold I Bluetooth (ruled about 940–985), while at the end of the century Olof Skötkonung (died 1022) unified the two major tribes of Sweden—the Svear and the Götar.

RISE OF DENMARK

Denmark was to become the strongest and most powerful of these three nations. Harold soon conquered Norway, and by the time his grandson

Canute I (died 1035) inherited the Danish crown in 1019, the Danish empire included a large part of England as well. For much of the rest of the Middle Ages Denmark was the dominant state in Scandinavia, but the political situation in the region constantly changed as new rulers gained power.

One of the biggest developments to occur to Scandinavia in the 11th century was the establishment of Christianity as the region's major religion. An important distinguishing characteristic of Scandinavian culture was the fact that for many years the area had remained pagan, while the rest of western Europe was Christian. Missionaries such as Saint Ansgar (about 801–865) had tried to convert the inhabitants of the area as early as the ninth century, but with little success. Even those people who accepted Christianity often worshiped the Christian God alongside their traditional deities.

Slowly the situation started to change. By the 10th century Norway,

ICELAND AND GREENLAND

During the ninth century a group of Vikings discovered Iceland when they were blown off course on their way to the islands of the Hebrides. Around 870 the first settlers went to Iceland from Norway, and within 60 years nearly all the good farming land had been claimed and settled. Unlike the rest of Scandinavia, there was no king in Iceland, and in 930 the colonists set up an annual assembly called the Althing. It is usually regarded as the world's first parliament. Only tribal chieftains could vote at the assembly, which made laws for the island's 25,000 inhabitants.

By this time some Vikings had sailed further west and sighted another, much larger island. Around 983 a Norwegian named Erik the Red found summer grass growing near the shore of the huge island and named it Greenland. He hoped that this name would attract settlers from Iceland, and three years later he returned with a number of Viking longships. Over the next 200 years the Scandinavians set up hundreds of farms, and their colonies grew to hold up to 4,000 people. In 1261 the Greenlanders agreed to come under Norwegian rule, and two years later the Icelanders did the same.

This reconstruction of a traditional Viking house is based on the remains of an original building found at Stöng, Iceland. The remains date back to the Viking colonization of the island in the ninth century. The building has no windows, and the roof is covered in turf as a protection against the cold.

HEDEBY

Hedeby, on the Jutland peninsula near Schleswig (in present-day Germany), was one of the most important of the early Scandinavian coastal towns. Danish merchants settled there at the beginning of the ninth century. The settlement's craftsmen worked in metal, bone, glass, and amber. Ships were also repaired near the harbor, where Viking trading ships moored to deliver and collect the merchants' goods. Hedeby was the first Scandinavian town to mint coins, a fact that showed its importance as a trading settlement. At its peak around 950 the town was home to more than 1,000 people, who lived in wooden houses with roofs covered in thatch or turf. Hedeby's defenses were linked to the Dannevirke rampart. By 1100 falling sea levels meant that larger merchant ships found it difficult to use the harbor at Hedeby, and the town was abandoned.

A 12th-century stave church in Borgund, Norway. The distinctive design of the stave church was probably based on that of earlier pagan temples.

Sweden, and Denmark were all governed by Christian kings, and by the 11th century Scandinavia was largely Christian. Gradually the area developed closer links to the rest of western Europe in other respects as well. Several Scandinavian trading towns started to develop close ties with their counterparts in Germany. Eventually, in the 13th and 14th centuries towns such as Bergen in Norway would become important members of the Hanseatic League, an organization that dominated northern European trade.

A UNITED SCANDINAVIA

By the end of the 14th century Scandinavia had achieved a lasting unity. In 1363 a 10-year-old Danish princess named Margaret (1353–1412) married King Haakon VI of Norway. Margaret acted as regent for her young son Olaf when first her father and then her husband died. When Olaf also died, in 1387, Margaret became queen of both Denmark and Norway. Eight years later Swedish nobles turned to her for military help, and in 1397 the three

Scandinavian kingdoms were united under Queen Margaret by a treaty called the Union of Kalmar. This made Scandinavia a united region at the end of the Middle Ages.

SCHOLASTICISM

Scholasticism is the term that describes the method used to teach theology (religious thought) and philosophy (which attempts to explain human life and its problems) in cathedral schools and European universities between about 1050 and 1450. The main aim of scholastics was to reconcile faith and reason by means of logical questions and answers. They presented their views in the form of written commentaries, questions, and summaries.

During the Middle Ages Christian thinkers began from the assumption that the teachings of Christianity relating to creation and the natural world and God and the spiritual world were true. Their problem was whether one simply had to believe them (faith), or whether they could be proved by reason (logical argument). All their efforts were concentrated on proving that faith and reason were compatible.

Until the 12th century the education given in monastic schools was largely based on the work of Augustine, bishop of Hippo (354–430). He taught that because all knowledge is in the mind of God, it forms a unified system. This means that truth revealed by God is not in conflict with human reason.

The sixth-century scholar Boethius is sometimes called the founder of scholasticism because of the last sentence in one of his works: "As far as you are able, join faith to reason." This command formed the basis of scholasticism. Toward the middle of the 11th century Anselm, archbishop of Canterbury (about 1033–1109), set about proving by logic the existence of God. He argued that a Christian had a duty to understand faith through the reasoning of philosophy.

Scholastic method consisted of asking a general question (for example, "Is the world created or eternal?"), citing "authorities" who gave different answers (the Bible, ancient philosophers), and then attempting to reconcile these apparently contradictory answers through logical analysis.

EARLY SCHOLASTICS

The two most outstanding early scholastics were Peter Abelard (about 1079–1144) and Peter Lombard (about 1095–1160). Abelard's major work, *Yes and No*, set out contradictory statements drawn from biblical teachings. His students were asked to reconcile them through logical argument. Lombard compiled a summary of Christian ideas, the *Four Books of Sentences*, that became a standard text in universities.

Although some ancient Greek philosophers like Aristotle were studied during the early Middle Ages

This 15th-century stained-glass window from the Cathedral of Notre Dame in Tournai, France, shows Anselm of Laon (died 1117) being ordained as bishop. He studied under Anselm of Canterbury and became a noted early scholastic.

ISLAMIC INFLUENCE

Muslims had long had Arabic translations of Greek science and philosophy. The philosophies taught by the Islamic scholars Avicenna (980–1037) and al-Ghazali (1058–1111) mingled with the theology of traditional Islam, Judaism, and Christianity, provoking lively discussion. At the University of Córdoba in Spain the most influential philosopher was Averroës (1126–1198), whose study of Aristotle had led him to the conclusion that faith and reason provide two separate bodies of truth, equally valid but irreconcilable. When the works of Aristotle and Averroës were translated into Latin, they had a considerable effect on the scholastics. Some, such as Siger of Brabant (about 1240–1282), eagerly adopted Averroës' "two truths" as an excellent solution to intellectual dilemmas, while others, such as Thomas Aquinas, forcefully opposed it.

A 14th-century fresco, or wall painting, of Albertus Magnus (about 1200–1280), who taught at Cologne in Germany and in Paris. He was a renowned scholar. *Magnus* means "the Great" in Latin.

in monastic schools, around 1200 more of Aristotle's works were discovered, and others were first translated into Latin from Arabic. Arabic commentaries on Aristotle reached western Europe at the same time (see box). From then on, scholastics focused almost entirely on Aristotle. He had taught that all human knowledge is based on what we experience physically, and that by our power of reason we are able to build up an understanding of truth.

Many of Aristotle's ideas, such as the eternity of the world, posed a direct challenge to Christian beliefs based on the revelation from God in the Bible.

Two Dominican scholars dedicated their lives to reconciling Christianity and the Aristotelian system. Albertus Magnus (about 1200–1280) wrote 21 volumes of commentary on Aristotle. His student, Thomas Aquinas (about 1225–1274), is most famous for his *Summa Theologiae*. It grapples with the problem that if all knowledge is based on what we experience physically, how can we ever know God, who is not physical? His answer was that truths can be reached both through faith and reason.

Dominican scholasticism was opposed by the Franciscans. John Duns Scotus (about 1266–1308) questioned whether reason and faith could be combined. His pupil, William of Ockham (about 1285–1349), argued that knowledge and faith were separate and that bringing the two together was not possible or even desirable. Eventually most scholars began to agree with William of Ockham, and by the 15th century scholasticism had been replaced by new problems and questions.

SCIENCE AND MATHEMATICS

Science is the systematic attempt to understand the world of nature by using observation and reason. Compared to the great period of ancient Greek philosophy and science and the beginnings of modern science in the 16th and 17th centuries, the Middle Ages was not, on the whole, a time of great advancement, especially in western Europe. China made many discoveries between the third and 13th centuries, while Arab scientists and mathematicians were responsible for rescuing many works of the ancient Greeks from obscurity. Arab thinkers also made significant advances of their own.

This 13th-century image shows God as the architect of the world.

The Arabs regarded science as vitally important. Muhammad (about 570–632), the founder of Islam, had particularly praised medicine, and astronomy and astrology were believed to indicate God's will. By the ninth century Arab scholars had translated the major works of ancient Greece and were beginning to develop their own ideas. To work out the positions of the stars, they developed trigonometry, building logarithmic tables that are still used today. They also constructed the first "modern" astronomical observatories that used instruments to measure heavenly bodies, such as planets and stars, and created star

A Muslim pharmacist makes up a medicine in this 13th-century illustration. The experiments of Arab alchemists led to the development of medical chemistry, or pharmacy.

tables from their observations. They adopted what we call "Arabic" numerals from India, including zero and the decimal system. The most important Arab mathematician was al-Khwarizmi (about 780–850). Through his writings knowledge of algebra and the decimal system eventually reached Italy and then spread throughout Europe. The discovery of Chinese papermaking methods vastly improved and speeded up the spread of knowledge.

THE STUDY OF LIGHT

The greatest achievement of the Arabs lay in the field of optics, which is the name for the study of light. Ibn al-Haytham, or Alhazen (965–1039), who lived in Egypt, wrote a very comprehensive and influential book on optics, which was translated into Latin in 1270. He was the first person to give an accurate description of how the eye sees things.

The Greeks had believed that the eye gave out light in order to see objects. Alhazen argued, correctly, that the eye sees by receiving light from objects. He was a true scientist, who dissected eyes in order to find out whether their structure fitted in with this theory. He found the lens at the front of the eye, which concentrated light on a screen, called the retina, at the back. He also discovered that the retina was connected to the brain by an optic nerve. Alhazen's discoveries laid the foundations for the development of optical instruments, including, centuries later, the telescope.

CHRISTIAN SCIENCE

Why was there such a long pause in the development of scientific knowledge in the West? Part of the answer lies with the Romans, the successors to the Greek rulers of the Mediterranean world. Preoccupied

ALCHEMY

Alchemy, the supposed science of changing base metals (especially lead) into gold, fired men's imaginations from the time of ancient Greece and China down to the 17th century. In the early Middle Ages alchemy was largely an Arab pursuit—the word comes from the Arabic *al-kimiya*, meaning "the art of transmutation." The Arabs learned of it from a fourth-century Egyptian treatise.

Alchemists searched for a rumored substance that could turn lead into gold. They called it the Philosopher's Stone. No one, of course, ever found it. But the belief in alchemy, which the Arabs transmitted to Europe in the 12th century, did not subside. Alchemists concocted strange recipes of sulfur, copper, and mercury in their laboratories or heated metals until they glittered like gold. Gullible people were taken in by charlatans who claimed to have found the secret. Although alchemy was more superstition than science, alchemists discovered important substances such as distilled alcohol, accumulated valuable knowledge about alloys (mixtures of two or more metals), and invented many pieces of equipment for heating and distillation that were useful for later scientific experiments.

This 16th-century illustration shows an alchemist and his assistant heating an experimental mixture.

Closely related to the Philosopher's Stone was the search for a magic cure for all ills, or the "elixir" of life. Alchemists tried many combinations of metals, produced by heating and vaporization, in the effort to manufacture a substance that would prolong life indefinitely. A Swiss physician called Paracelsus, who had studied alchemy at Basel University, claimed to have found the answer—wine in which some of the Philosopher's Stone had been dissolved. He died in 1541—at the age of only 47.

with the building of a vast empire and with the practical problems of governing it, they spent little time on the pursuit of knowledge itself. Even more important was the influence of Christianity. Science concerns itself with the visible evidence of things. Greek scientists working before the coming of Christianity had observed things in the natural world, then described and measured them in the hope of understanding how they worked. Christians, however, saw science as a means of understanding God's creation and therefore of understanding God.

In place of arguments about how things on this earth worked, early medieval scholars spent their energies on disputes about the nature of God and the fine points of Christian belief, or dogma. Nevertheless, scientific observation and the recording of knowledge continued to take place.

Belief in astrology—despite the opposition of theologians such as Saint Augustine of Hippo (354–430)—meant that observation of the heavens continued. Because of the need to celebrate church festivals on the proper day (especially Easter), great effort was given to calendrical calculations. The standard work on this subject was written by the seventh-century Anglo-Saxon monk Bede (about 673–735). Medicinal herbal remedies were concocted in monasteries, and for practical reasons the careful recording of observations and knowledge concerning plants and animals continued throughout the Middle Ages.

EUROPEAN REVIVAL

The Islamic world's interest in science meant that Greek knowledge finally reached Europe. Translations included Euclid's major work on geometry, *Elements*, the works of the inventor and mathematician Archimedes, and al-Kwarizmi's treatises on algebra and arithmetic. From the 11th century

CHINESE SCIENCE

Unlike almost all other ancient peoples, the Chinese did not believe that gods, demons, and spirits influenced events. They believed that the universe was ordered and that humans had a duty to discover this order and use it effectively. Emperors and their officials encouraged science in the expectation that it would be used to create new technology that would improve efficiency. The emphasis was on practical science, such as improvements in agriculture, engineering, transportation, and warfare.

As a result China invented many things centuries before western Europe, such as paper, cast iron, gunpowder, the waterwheel, using coal as fuel, lacquer, porcelain, distillation, kites, suspension bridges, and seismographs for detecting earthquakes—to mention just a few. One of the greatest Chinese medieval scientists, Shen Kua (about 1031–1095), wrote a famous book called *Dream Pool Essays* that for the first time described

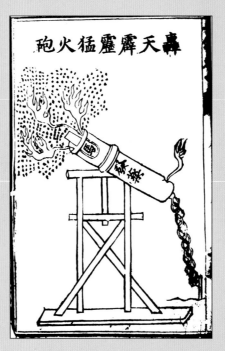

磞火猛霹靂天轟

magnetic compasses and movable type, and gave accurate descriptions of fossils. The book also discusses astronomy, optics, mathematics, and mapmaking. Not until the 16th century would Europe reach the same level of achievement.

Having gained this huge lead in science and technology, however, progress came to a halt in the 14th century, when a change in attitude meant that Chinese rulers, and therefore their officials, no longer encouraged innovation. Many inventions fell into disuse, while others were forgotten. When a European scholar brought a mechanical clock to China in 1600, everyone was amazed, quite unaware that it had first been invented in eighth-century China.

The Chinese were the first to use poison gas in warfare by mixing the poison arsenic into gunpowder. This medieval weapon was called "the heaven-rumbling fierce fire erupter."

onward, alongside the revival of the European economy, the growth of towns, and the establishment of the first universities at places like Padua, Paris, and Oxford, there were the beginnings of a revival of intellectual curiosity about the world.

Foremost in starting that revival was the Cathedral School at Chartres, just south of Paris. Thierry of Chartres (about 1100–1156) declared that "on mathematics all rational explanation of the universe depended." Two English scholars, Robert Grosseteste (about 1175–1253) and Roger Bacon (about 1220–1292), asserted the same faith in the powers of human observation, scientific experiment, and reason. Both made valuable contributions to the study of light and optics.

According to the Bible, light was one of the first creations of God, so Christian scholars believed that understanding light would help explain the nature of the universe. They tried, for example, to explain the colors of the rainbow by simulating the conditions that created rainbows in their studios, using glass bowls filled with water.

ARISTOTLE'S WRITINGS

This scientific view of the world as explainable by observation and reason was derived above all from the writings of the ancient Greek philosopher Aristotle (about 384–322 B.C.). Many scientists and philosophers tried to find a way to reconcile the teachings of the church with the scientific views of Aristotle. This meant bringing faith and reason together.

The attempt alarmed some theologians, or religious thinkers. The teaching of Aristotle was banned at the University of Paris in 1210,

though without long-term effect, and many universities followed its example. In 1277 the bishop of Paris condemned 219 "execrable errors" of Aristotle. The effect of that condemnation was to lead some philosophers to completely separate science and faith.

Many advances in the study of logic were made in the 14th century, and many Aristotelian views were criticized in the 15th century. Ironically, Aristotle became the official philosopher of the church in the 16th century, and his ideas were used to condemn scientists such as Galileo (1564–1642), who claimed that his observations of the skies confirmed that the earth went around the sun.

Roger Bacon, a Franciscan scholar and scientist.

SEE ALSO

♦ Astronomy
♦ Calendars and Clocks
♦ Islamic Scholarship
♦ Paper and Printing
♦ Religious Thought and Philosophy
♦ Scholasticism
♦ Tools and Technology
♦ Universities

SCOTLAND

Scotland occupies the northern part of the British Isles and consists of mountainous highlands in the north and more fertile lowlands in the south. It became an independent kingdom in the ninth century, when the most powerful peoples who lived there, the Picts and Scots, came together. From this time Scotland's history was marked by struggles for the throne and for independence from its powerful neighbor to the south, England.

Several different peoples lived in the north of Britain during the early medieval period. In the north were the Picts, who got their name from the Latin word *picti*, which means "painted ones," because they painted or tattooed their skin. Britons lived in the southwest, and Angles from Germany lived in the southeast. In the late fifth century people from northern Ireland called Scots colonized the west coast. An Irish missionary named Columba founded a monastery on the Scottish

A 15th-century illustration of the Battle of Neville's Cross (1346) in which King David II of Scotland (1324–1371) was captured by the English. It was one of many battles fought between the Scottish and English.

island of Iona in 565 and began to convert Scotland to Christianity. In the 790s Viking raiders from Norway began to invade and by the mid-ninth century had settled western and northern coastal regions.

People from Scottish and Pictish families began marrying each other during the eighth century. In 843 Kenneth MacAlpin, king of the Scots, took over control of the Picts and created the first united kingdom in Scotland, known as Alba. Powerful family units played an important part in Scottish society, particularly in the remote highlands, where they were called clans.

POWER STRUGGLES

There were many violent struggles for the Scottish throne. In 1040, for example, King Duncan I's claim was challenged by his cousin Macbeth, a chief from northern Scotland. Macbeth killed Duncan in a battle at Elgin and held the crown until his death in 1057. The playwright William Shakespeare based his play *Macbeth* on a 16th-century account of his life.

After the Norman Conquest of England in 1066 Scottish kings welcomed powerful Norman knights and nobles, whom they used to strengthen their rule. They gave the

WILLIAM WALLACE

William Wallace (about 1270–1305) was a Scottish soldier whose revolt against King Edward I made him a national hero. In 1297 Wallace led a group of men who killed the English sheriff—whom Edward had appointed to enforce his rule—drove the English out of Scotland, and raided northern England. He became guardian of the Scottish kingdom in the name of John de Baliol, who had been imprisoned. Edward led an army of armored knights and longbowmen against the rebels and defeated Wallace at Falkirk in 1298. Wallace escaped and went to France to ask for help, before returning to Scotland to carry on the fight. In 1305 he was captured, taken to London, and executed for treason.

Normans land in return for their support, establishing a feudal system in the lowlands, although the clans remained powerful in the highlands.

BATTLES WITH ENGLAND

The Scottish kings constantly struggled to remain independent from the English, and in 1290 the situation became critical when the successor to the Scottish throne, Margaret, died. Thirteen Scottish nobles claimed the right to succeed her; King Edward I of England supported John de Baliol but also took advantage of the disorder to try to establish direct rule.

The Scottish rebelled against Edward's rule, led first by William Wallace and then by Robert Bruce, one of the 13 nobles who had made a claim to the throne. Robert Bruce defeated Edward II in the Battle of Bannockburn in 1314, and the English finally recognized him as Robert I, king of the Scots, in 1328.

Despite this, hostilities continued, and more battles were fought against the English, the Scots suffering a serious defeat at Halidon Hill in 1333. But England's attention soon turned away from Scotland to the Hundred Years' War with France.

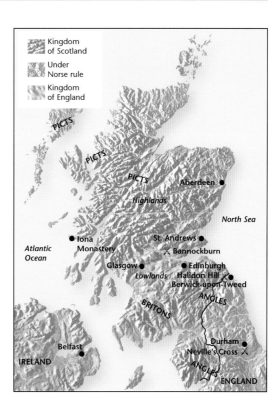

A map showing the kingdom of Scotland around 1000. After repeated Viking raids from the end of the eighth century the west coast and islands were under Norse rule. To the south the border with England was fought over for centuries.

When Robert I's son David died in 1371, the house of Stuart came to the throne. Scotland enjoyed a period of relative stability, although fighting continued along the English border, where powerful Scottish and English families (such as the Douglases and Percys) fought for possession of land. The arts flourished, and in the 15th century universities were founded at St. Andrews, Glasgow, and Aberdeen.

SEE ALSO

♦ Edward I
♦ England
♦ Feudalism
♦ Missionaries
♦ Vikings

This modern illustration shows a Viking dragon-ship under sail. Shutters sealed the oar holes when the oars were not in use. The large rectangular, colored sail was woven from a double thickness of raw woolen cloth.

SHIPS AND SEAFARING

The ships of Europe were shaped by conditions in two very different oceans. The boats of northern Europe had to contend with strong winds, heavy seas, tides, and shallows, while the minimal tides and moderate summer winds of the Mediterranean produced a very different kind of craft. Both were influenced by Arab and Chinese developments in shipbuilding and seafaring that gradually spread to Europe.

The Vikings of Scandinavia were expert sailors. They braved the stormy North and Baltic Seas, and even crossed the Atlantic Ocean to North America. They dominated the northern seas from the eighth to the late 11th century. We know about Viking shipbuilding techniques because their leaders were sometimes buried in boats, which were then preserved. Vikings took to the sea for both peaceful and warlike purposes. They used ships on raiding parties to plunder coastal towns, on trading missions, and to explore and colonize distant new lands.

Viking ships had several features that were common to all north

European ships. The hull was made of overlapping oak planks nailed together in a technique called clinker-building and fastened to oak ribs. This formed a strong double-ended hull that could stand up to northern seas. A shallow keel that ran down the underside of the ship helped keep it stable. Sailors steered with a special oar lashed to the right-hand side near the stern. There was a single mast with a large rectangular sail made of cloth. In calmer weather the ship was powered by 16 to 30 oarsmen on each side.

The Vikings built two main kinds of boats, longships and *knörrs*. Longships were swift, slim boats up to

LIVING CONDITIONS

Conditions were appalling on medieval ships, particularly on long voyages. Food was usually poor even when fresh; on long trips maggots and weevils infested grains and meat. Drinking water was stagnant and often in short supply. Partly because of the poor diet, illnesses such as dysentery and scurvy were common. Hygiene and sanitation were also poor, and conditions very cramped. Men slept on the planking—hammocks were unknown until Columbus saw them in use in the New World.

Viking ships were open to the elements. Sailors sat on their sea chests to row. In stormy northern waters they must have spent most of the time drenched and cold. Sagas relate that while half the men rowed, the other half baled out water. Caravels and carracks had tall masts that towered high above deck. Climbing them to adjust the rigging was a dangerous task, especially in stormy weather. It was not uncommon for sailors to fall to their death or be swept overboard by waves.

100 ft. (30m) long. They were used for war and piracy. Known as *drakkars*, or dragon-ships, they sometimes had a fierce dragon's or snake's head carved on the high prow. *Knörrs* were shorter and deeper. They were used to ferry livestock and passengers, including colonists of new lands.

ARAB DHOWS

The Arabs were also practiced seafarers. Around the same time as the Vikings, their ships sailed the length of the Mediterranean, calling at Muslim colonies in North Africa and Spain. By the 13th century Arab ships were venturing down the east coast of Africa and east to China and the East Indies on trading missions.

Arab boats, called dhows, were very different from Viking longships. For a start, Arab shipbuilders used no nails to fasten the planks of the ship's hull; instead, timbers were lashed together with strands of coconut fiber. Some dhows had two or even three masts and were rigged with triangular lateen sails on a long spar. They allowed Arab craft to sail almost into the wind, which Viking ships could not. A hinged rudder attached to the stern

made the boats easy to steer. They were built to sail in the steady northeast monsoon winds of the Indian Ocean; during the stormy southwest monsoon they would be laid up on a beach or in port.

CHINESE JUNKS

While Arab dhows tacked across the Mediterranean Sea and the Indian Ocean, Chinese and Japanese mariners sailed the coastal Pacific Ocean in giant ships called junks. Venetian

The sails of this modern junk have not changed since medieval times. Sails are reduced in area or lowered by a single rope that folds the sails up like an accordion. This is much easier and quicker than the western rig.

traveler Marco Polo was amazed by their size when he visited China in the late 13th century. "Most have at least 60 cabins, each of which can comfortably accommodate one merchant," he wrote. Some junks measured up to 180 ft. (55m) long. Their stout hulls were made of two layers of planks nailed together. Below-deck bulkheads divided the hull into watertight sections, which prevented the whole ship from flooding if it was holed.

Junks had up to six masts, which carried huge square sails made of matting and stiffened with bamboo slats. They made it easy to reduce sail in bad weather. They were also easy to steer, since the Chinese had developed the stern rudder as early as the fourth century B.C. Their ships were mainly used for trading in coastal waters, but in the early 15th century a fleet of junks under the command of Admiral Cheng Ho explored the Indian Ocean as far as the coast of East Africa.

NORTHERN COGS

After the Viking era ended around 1070, the shipbuilders of northern Europe continued to use the longship design for another century or so. By the 13th century, however, a new kind of ship, the cog, had been developed. It was used to carry goods such as wool, wine, iron, and livestock between wealthy north German ports. Like Viking ships, cogs were clinker-

Archers and trumpet blowers prepare for action in this 14th-century illustration of a northern cog.

NAVIGATION

Medieval mariners had few navigation aids to help them find their way. Ships usually kept close to shore, so sailors could look out for familiar landmarks. Out on the open ocean it was all too easy to get lost. Skillful seamen watched waves and currents, and used the sun, moon, and stars to locate their position. Often, however, clouds hid these guides from view. Time was kept by a half-hour sandglass, which had to be constantly turned.

Viking sailors used a device like a sundial to measure the sun's position at midday. Using special tables, they could then work out their latitude (distance north or south). Arab mariners used a tool called a *kamal* to measure the height of certain stars above the horizon. They also improved astrolabes, working models of the heavens, that had been invented by the ancient Greeks.

By 1200 Chinese, European, and Arab mariners were all using magnetic compasses for navigation. Historians believe that each culture may have discovered independently that a magnetized needle would rotate to point north when suspended on a string or floated in water. Captains kept records of their voyages, which developed into the portolano, a coastal pilot book for harbor-finding. The information in these books was used to draw up the first marine charts, called portolans. They were hand drawn and so very expensive.

A 15th-century illustration shows a fleet of carracks preparing to pick up French soldiers who are setting off on the Third Crusade (1189–1192). The triangular projecting bow was called a "carrack bow" and gave the boat its name.

built, with a single large square sail. However, they were broader and deeper than longships, with a deck built over the hull and a rudder attached to the stern. Structures called castles were built at the prow and stern. The forecastle carried soldiers to defend the boat against pirates and other enemies. The sterncastle protected passengers from the elements. This sturdy design lasted for about 200 years.

CARRACKS AND CARAVELS

While cogs sailed northern waters, other kinds of craft were being developed in the shipyards of Italy, Portugal, and Spain. They used lateen sails, like Arab dhows, which made them easy to maneuver. Unlike cogs, they were built by nailing planks edge to edge onto a stout wooden frame, a new technique called carvel-building.

By the mid-15th century Mediterranean shipbuilders were combining the best features of cogs and lateen craft to build fast, easily maneuvered boats called caravels. These full-rigged ships had three masts and carried a mixture of lateen and square sails, which meant they could perform well in different conditions. Caravels had forecastles and sterncastles, and were steered with rudders.

Carracks were larger craft that developed around the same time. They were used as storeships and later as battleships. Both of these craft were used on voyages of discovery. During the early 15th century Portuguese caravels explored the west coast of Africa. In 1492 Christopher Columbus reached the shores of North America in a carrack, the *Santa Maria*, and two caravels.

SEE ALSO

♦ Exploration
♦ Islamic Empire
♦ Maps and
   Mapmakers
♦ Marco Polo
♦ Trade
♦ Vikings
♦ Warfare

SLAVES AND SLAVERY

Slavery was commonplace in most societies during the Middle Ages and was regarded as a normal part of life. Agricultural slavery gradually declined in Europe because nobles were able to use peasant labor and rents from land to support their way of life. Domestic slavery continued, however, to the end of the Middle Ages. In the 15th and 16th centuries slavery almost completely disappeared from Europe but was being re-created on the Canary Islands and in the New World. In many other parts of the world, such as India and China, it continued to play a significant role.

A slave was a person who was owned by someone else—an individual or a state. A slave could be bought, sold, or given away. A slave received no pay for his or her labor. The owner had the right to separate a slave from his or her family members and controlled slaves' rights to marry, their freedom of movement, and their activities. Slaves did not have the same legal protections as free persons, although special regulations usually governed their treatment. Slaves generally came from a different ethnic group, race, or religion than their owners.

SOURCES OF SLAVES

Wars produced the most slaves. The victors had total power over the defeated and could either kill them, take them as slaves, or sell them to slave traders. Pirates and raiders such as the Vikings took captives to sell into slavery in addition to their other plunder. After war the biggest source of slaves was children born to slave women. In addition, some people were made slaves as a punishment for crimes, children were sold into slavery by their parents or other relatives as payment for debts or so they would

This statue, called the *Young Slave*, was carved by Michelangelo (1475–1564). It was one of four statues of slaves intended for the tomb of Pope Julius II, but never completed. The twisted body conveys terror and grief, and seems to be struggling to free itself from the marble.

escape hunger, and people even sold themselves into slavery to escape starvation or bad debts.

SLAVES IN SOCIETY

Ancient Greece and Rome were both slave-owning civilizations. When the western Roman Empire finally fell in the fifth century, slavery began to evolve into serfdom. Agricultural slaves were replaced by *coloni*, or tenant farmers. The conditions of the *coloni* were not much better than those of slaves because they remained permanently in debt to the landowner. *Coloni*, therefore, were the forerunners of serfs. A serf gave labor and rent in return for the protection of the lord of the manor and a piece of land to farm for himself and his family.

Some historians have compared serfdom with slavery; but although serf comes from *servus*, the Latin word for slave, and the serf's situation was often not much better than that of a slave, there were important differences. Slaves were employed in many different occupations, whereas serfs worked on the land and were bound to the land instead of to an individual owner. In addition, serfs had some legal rights: They could own property. The lord did not

SLAVE TRADE

During the Middle Ages slaves came from four main sources—the Slavs (the origin of "slave") in eastern Europe, farmers in southern Persia, sub-Saharan Africans, and Celtic, Germanic, and Gallic peoples. Settled agricultural societies were most in danger of being raided by wandering nomadic societies and taken as slaves. In the fifth century the Huns from Central Asia and a Germanic tribe called the Vandals made brutal raids on western Europe and carried off slaves as part of their booty. Between the ninth and 11th centuries the Vikings raided far and wide in search of plunder and slaves. In the 13th century the Central Asian Mongols raided China, Russia, the Middle East, and eastern Europe, and then sold slaves throughout Asia.

The slave trade was a profitable enterprise, and extensive trade networks spread through Africa and Europe. The Arabs took slaves from the island of Zanzibar, East Africa, Sudan, Ethiopia, and the Sahara, transported them across the Red Sea and the Indian Ocean, and sold them throughout the Islamic Empire. The Venetians and Genoese dominated the slave trade in the Mediterranean. Other networks built up across Asia and Europe. The Ottoman Empire, in particular, bought large numbers of slaves from eastern Europe and Africa.

Traders used this room on the island of Zanzibar to hold slaves before they were sent to market.

dictate their family life, and serfs could, through hard work and luck, buy their land and change their status to that of a free man or woman. It was also possible for peasants to move to new land if they were oppressed by their overlords.

Slavery seemed natural in a society that was very structured. People were born into a particular class, and the majority tended to stay there. Most men followed the professions of their fathers. Christianity did not forbid slavery, although the church tried to protect the rights of slaves.

The Bible described slavery as God's punishment for sin, and Augustine of Hippo (354–430), in *The City of God*, argued that slavery was justified because slaves were inferior to their masters: "The justice of masters dominating slaves is clear,

because those who excel in reason should excel in power." Christians, therefore, owned and bought slaves, particularly to work in the household.

All Islamic societies owned slaves. Islamic law (*Shari'a*) covered the legal aspects of owning slavery in detail— from obtaining slaves to keeping or freeing them. No follower of Islam could be made a slave by another Muslim. Slave owners were expected to free their slaves after a number of years, particularly if the slave had converted to Islam. These two factors meant that Islamic societies had a continual need to obtain new slaves from other societies.

AFRICA AND ASIA

Slavery was an accepted way of life in Asian and African countries. Slavery is known to have existed during the

A 13th-century illustration of a slave market in Yemen. In the top half of the picture a merchant weighs a gold coin so that he can make a sale; the bottom half shows a Muslim man selecting new servants.

SLAVE OCCUPATIONS

The majority of slaves were used for domestic or agricultural labor. House slaves served in the home, doing the cooking and cleaning, and looking after their owner's children. They were often a status symbol, demonstrating their owner's wealth. Slaves were popular if crops were labor-intensive—harvesting olives, grapes, sugar, and cotton, and planting and tending rice—or in occupations such as mining, where the work was hard and dangerous. Women slaves were often forced into prostitution or became concubines (unmarried wives), expected to produce children for their owner.

A small number of slaves moved into more prestigious occupations. Slaves who fought as soldiers tended to be more highly regarded. The Egyptian Mamluks and the Ottoman Janissaries were troops of professional slave soldiers who became involved in struggles for political power. The Mamluks eventually rose in rebellion against the Egyptian caliph in the 13th century and became the rulers of Egypt. In the Islamic world slaves often became merchants. Long-distance trading caravans were frequently under the command of a slave, who was entrusted with large sums of money and many valuable goods.

Shang dynasty (1766–1100 B.C.) in China and continued to be part of Chinese life until the 20th century. However, because China has always had a large population who needed work, slaves were never numerous.

Korea, on the other hand, had a particularly large number of slaves —from the end of the Silla period in 918 to the mid-18th century between a third and a half of the population were slaves. There were also large numbers of slaves in India, most of whom came from the local population. This is because castes, or classes, were very important in India, and the owners wanted slaves who belonged to certain castes.

Slaves have been owned in Africa throughout recorded history. But the numbers increased as the Islamic Empire expanded. Soon black slaves were being widely traded throughout the Islamic world.

Throughout history slaves have tried to escape or rebel. Rates of escape varied from society to society. In places like Russia, however, where slaves were often natives or of similar origin and there was an open frontier, as many as a third of slaves ran away. The best-known medieval slave rebellion took place in Iraq in the ninth century and lasted for 14 years.

The persistence of slavery in the Middle Ages was largely due to the clash of very different cultures and religions, especially during the Crusades. Muslims and Christians both enslaved captives taken after battles. Muslim pirates in the Mediterranean enslaved Christian passengers and sailors captured in raids on shipping. This was such a frequent occurrence that Christians began to form organizations to seek the slaves' release by force or ransom.

In northern Europe slavery began to disappear as pagans were converted to Christianity and contacts with non-Christians ended. Between the ninth and 12th centuries slavery declined in most of Europe as serfs took their place. Mediterranean countries, however, kept slaves, mostly black, until the mid-16th century.

SLAVIC PEOPLES

In the Middle Ages the Slavs were the largest group of people in Europe who shared a common ethnic origin and language. They were mainly based in east and southeast Europe, and were divided into three broad groupings: West Slavs, comprising Poles, Slovaks, Wends, and Czechs; East Slavs, comprising Russians, Belarussians, and Ukrainians; and South Slavs, comprising Serbs, Bulgars, Macedonians, Slovenes, and Croats. The various Slavic peoples adopted separate national identities as Slavic states began forming and did not unite in any way.

The Slavs had originally migrated from Asia in about 2000 B.C. They were nomadic hunters and herders who wandered from place to place. Extended families lived together under the strict rule of a clan chieftain. They worshiped numerous gods and believed that forest spirits (*leshy*), water spirits (*vodyanov*), and house spirits (*domovoy*) would look favorably on offerings of bran and eggs.

MIGRATIONS

By the fifth and sixth centuries the Slavs had settled in the foothills of the Carpathian Mountains in eastern Europe, where they began to farm. In the late sixth and early seventh centuries they were overrun by nomadic invaders from Asia called the Avars. Constant pressure from the Avars pushed the Slavs westward into Bohemia, Slovakia, Hungary, Poland, Baltic and Finnish territory, eastward to the upper reaches of the Volga River, and southward into Macedonia, Greece, Croatia, Slovenia, Serbia, and Bulgaria.

As the Slavs settled, they began to form independent states led by princes and to marry into other

European cultures. Western Slavs gradually became European in outlook in that they experienced the economic, political, and intellectual changes taking place in western Europe during the Middle Ages. Russian and Baltic Slavs, however, had little contact with western Europe. Their social systems developed along quite different lines, becoming more military and dominated by state

Modern Russian Orthodox nuns take part in a procession at the Moscow Kremlin (built 1156) to celebrate Slavic written language and culture.

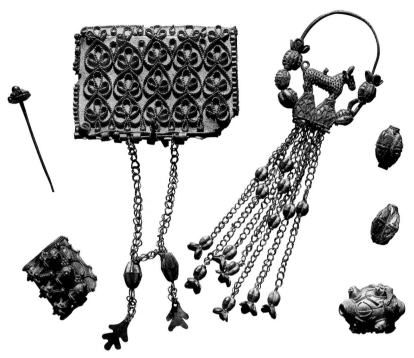

These finely worked items of silver jewelry come from the grave of a 10th-century Slavic princess and were found in the modern Czech Republic.

and Bulgars combined to raid the Byzantine Empire. When a Bulgar state formed in 681, its peoples and languages were essentially Slav. In the same year the Byzantine emperor recognized its independence.

CONVERSIONS

The Byzantine Empire wanted to convert the pagan Slavs to Eastern Orthodox Christianity. Photius, the patriarch, or bishop, enlisted the help of two brothers, Cyril and Methodius (see box). The missionaries of the Roman Catholic church in Rome resented their work, and the brothers came into conflict with the bishops of Salzburg and Passau, who were seeking to convert the western Slavs to Roman Catholic Christianity.

The conflict over the conversion of the Slavs deepened the growing rift between Rome and Constantinople, and permanently divided the Slavic peoples. Today Serbia and Bulgaria belong to the Eastern Orthodox church, while the Czechs, Slovenians, Slovaks, Hungarians, and Poles belong to the Roman Catholic faith.

bureaucracy. By the end of the Middle Ages many of the independent Slav states had collapsed, while others had been absorbed into larger states.

The first Slav state to emerge was Bulgaria. The Bulgars were not Slavs, but they intermarried with them and took on much of their culture. Slavs

CYRIL AND METHODIUS

Two brothers called Cyril (about 827–869) and Methodius (about 825–884) are known as the "apostles of the Slavs" because of their missionary work. Cyril was a professor of philosophy at Constantinople University. Methodius was an abbot of a Greek monastery. Both were linguists, scholars, and theologians. After a mission to the Khazars, a Central Asian people living near the Black Sea, they returned to Constantinople. In 863 the Byzantine emperor and the patriarch, or bishop, asked them to convert the southern Slavs. Believing that they would learn best from books in their own language, the brothers translated the scriptures into a language known as Old Church Slavonic and invented a Slavic alphabet of 40 letters based on Greek characters. Known as Cyrillic after Cyril, this alphabet in modified form is still used in Russia, Bulgaria, and Serbia. The brothers began their work in Moravia, and Christianity soon spread into Bulgaria and Serbia.

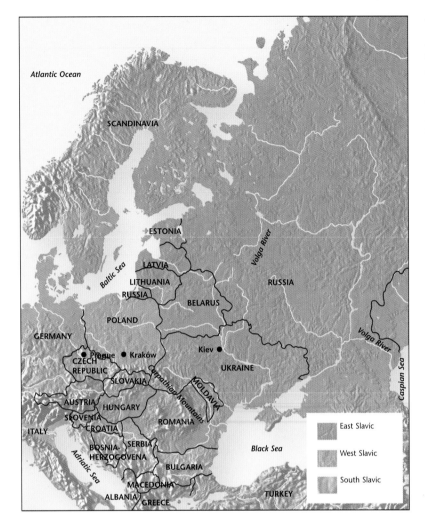

Atlantic Ocean

SCANDINAVIA

ESTONIA

LATVIA

LITHUANIA

RUSSIA

Baltic Sea

RUSSIA

BELARUS

Volga River

POLAND

GERMANY

Prague • Kraków • Kiev •

CZECH
REPUBLIC

SLOVAKIA

Volga River

Carpathian Mountains

MOLDAVIA

UKRAINE

Caspian Sea

AUSTRIA

HUNGARY

SLOVENIA

CROATIA

ROMANIA

ITALY

BOSNIA-
HERZOGOVENA

SERBIA

Black Sea

Adriatic Sea

BULGARIA

MACEDONIA

ALBANIA

GREECE

TURKEY

| East Slavic |
| West Slavic |
| South Slavic |

This map shows the distribution of the Slavic language groups in modern Europe. The borders of the Slavic states have changed constantly over the centuries and are still changing today.

RUSSIA AND POLAND

The Byzantine Empire particularly sought the conversion of the eastern Slavs of Russia. The Russians controlled the lucrative river trade routes between the Baltic Sea and the Black Sea, and made sporadic, savage raids on the Byzantine Empire. During the early 10th century the Byzantines made diplomatic and commercial contact with the Russians. Their policy paid off in 988, when Vladimir of Kiev was baptized into the Orthodox church. This led to the mass conversion of the Russian people, and Russia later became the main center of Eastern Orthodoxy. It also adopted the Cyrillic alphabet.

Poland began to take shape at about the same time as Russia. It too was a Slavic state, but its first ruler, Mieszko I (about 930–992), chose to adopt the Roman Catholic church. This meant that Poland became linked to the West, while Russia remained linked to the East. As the westernmost Slavic state, Poland faced continual waves of Germanic attack and migration. As the eastern-most Roman Catholic country, it bordered Orthodox Russia.

NEW STATES FORM

Other Slav peoples had been pushing into central Europe and began forming important states such as Bohemia and Moravia, which had been converted to Orthodox Christianity by Cyril and Methodius, but then became reconverted by the Germans to Roman Catholic Christianity. Croatia and Serbia also became separate states.

By the 12th century the Slavs were firmly established in Europe, although they had formed separate settlements and were divided by religion. The Magyars, who were not Slav, had also settled in the region that became Hungary. The strongest Slav power to emerge was Kievan Russia.

In the 13th century the western Slavic states came under increasing pressure from the Holy Roman Empire, which sought to dominate them economically and culturally. The military order of Teutonic Knights, which had invaded and conquered Prussia between 1233 and 1283, also became a serious threat to Slavic independence.

In 1237 the Mongols invaded eastern Europe. Kiev was destroyed in 1240, and the Russians had to pay tribute to them. It was only toward the end of the 14th century that Mongol power began to decline as the tribes fought among themselves.

GOOD KING WENCESLAS

Vaclav I, or Wenceslas (about 907–929), was raised as a Christian by his grandmother Ludmila, although his ambitious and scheming mother, Dragomir, was a pagan. After the death of his father in about 920 Dragomir became regent. When Vaclav became prince of Bohemia, his religious enthusiasm upset many Bohemians, who had not yet converted to Christianity.

In 929, when Germans invaded Bohemia, Vaclav submitted to the German king, Henry I. A group of nobles, enraged by his action, conspired against him, and his brother Boleslav had him murdered in the church doorway on his way to mass. Soon after his death rumors spread of miracles taking place at his tomb. An alarmed Boleslav had Vaclav's remains transferred to the church of St. Vitus in Prague, which soon became a place of pilgrimage. His feast day was celebrated from 985, and he became the patron saint of the Czech people. Wenceslas is also celebrated in the well-known 19th-century Christmas carol.

This portrait of Saint Wenceslas was painted in the 14th century on a wood panel.

PROSPERITY

In the 14th century western Europe suffered plagues, famines, and economic collapse, but the Slavic countries of the east flourished. In Bohemia Charles I (ruled 1346–1378) presided over a powerful state, its healthy economy owing much to the opening of silver mines in the 13th century and Prague's strategic position on east-west trade routes.

Poland benefited from trade with the Hanseatic League (a trading association of north German towns and cities) in the Baltic and exported large quantities of timber and grain to western Europe. The princes of eastern Europe called for settlers from the West, especially peasants from Germany and Flanders, to come east and help clear and settle new land, rebuild agriculture, and lay the foundations of new towns.

In the 12th century Lithuania had conquered large areas of Slav territory in Belarussia, Russia, and the Ukraine. In 1386 Jagiello, the grand duke of Lithuania, married Princess Jadwiga of Poland, uniting the two countries. In 1410 Jagiello's forces decisively defeated the Teutonic Knights at the Battle of Tannenberg.

For both Bohemia and Poland a decisive factor in their prosperity was the influx of German and Flemish settlers and their exploitation of the region's agricultural potential. The foundation of universities at Prague (1348) and Kraków (1364) reflects this new mood of cultural confidence.

SOUTHEAST ASIA

In the Middle Ages Southeast Asia was home to a number of flourishing kingdoms and empires. They were influenced by the older and more powerful Indian and Chinese cultures that lay to the northwest and northeast, but maintained their own distinct character.

Geographically, Southeast Asia consists of two distinct areas. The first is the wide mainland peninsula that is today made up of the countries Myanmar, Thailand, Laos, Cambodia, and Vietnam. The second consists of the narrow Malaysian Peninsula, the large islands of Java, Sumatra, and Borneo, and a vast number of smaller islands that extend from the Indian Ocean far out into the Pacific.

One of the most important geographical features of Southeast Asia is the number of large rivers, such as the Mekong, Salween, and Irrawaddy, that run through the mainland. During the rainy season these rivers flood the surrounding area, creating extremely fertile deltas that are ideal for growing rice. These ricefields can support large numbers of people.

KINGDOM OF FUNAN

The earliest recorded kingdom of Southeast Asia was Funan, located in the Mekong Delta region and peopled by the Khmer, ancestors of modern Cambodians. It was first mentioned in the records of a Chinese traveler in the third century A.D. and had apparently been in existence for several hundred years. Funan's capital was at Vyadhapura, near the later city of Phnom Penh.

Like all medieval Southeast Asian states, Funan was well situated for trade. It was located between the empires of India and China, and had many natural harbors. At the southern

A modern-day ricefield in Bali. The farmer uses a traditional plow.

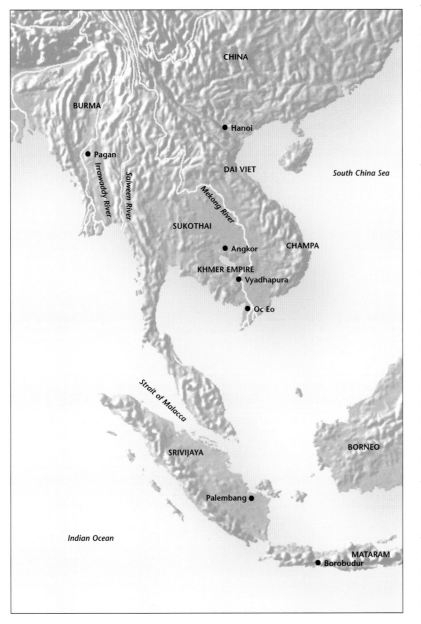

Vietnam and Thailand. It was founded by King Jayavarman II (about 790–850), who unified the Khmer peoples in defense against an invasion from Java. They successfully expelled the invaders and established a new capital city at Angkor, north of Tonle Sap Lake. Ruled by the Angkor dynasty, the empire endured for six centuries—between around 800 and 1400.

The Khmer Empire was heavily influenced by the culture of Gupta India. Evidence of this influence can be seen in the empire's art, architecture, poetry, mathematics, and use of Sanskrit. But the most enduring influence was Hinduism, brought by missionaries and adopted by the rajas (or rulers) as the state religion. The raja himself performed religious rituals, and the royal court financed the building of numerous temples throughout the country. The largest and most famous of these is Angkor Wat at Angkor.

BUDDHISM SPREADS

Although the official religion was Hinduism, Buddhism also gained many adherents, especially among the common people, who easily mixed it with their traditional forms of worship. The Bayon Temple, built in the 13th century, is Khmer's greatest Buddhist shrine. It is decorated with elaborate carvings that illustrate scenes from daily life.

Khmer's strength and wealth ensured that it was victorious in wars against its enemies in the east, Champa and Vietnam. The empire had good trading relations with China and resisted the payment of tribute to the Mongols in the 12th century. But as Mongol power engulfed most of Asia, it set in motion the migration of the Thai peoples from southwestern

This map shows the location of some of the main states that flourished in Southeast Asia in the Middle Ages.

tip of the country was the port of Oc Eo, from which Funanese merchants traveled in all directions, even as far as the Mediterranean.

THE KHMER EMPIRE

By the sixth century Funan was in decline. However, some 300 years later another Khmer state came into being. It was to prove the greatest of all the Southeast Asian states. At its height the Khmer Empire's territory covered all of modern Cambodia, as well as large parts of southern

ANGKOR WAT

The Khmer temple of Angkor Wat is one of the great architectural achievements of the medieval world. It was built in the 12th century under the orders of King Suryavarman II (ruled 1113–1150). The vast temple took 30 years to complete. Like other Khmer rulers, Suryavarman was seen as being a human incarnation of the god Vishnu. Angkor Wat was built as a temple to him and was intended to house his body when he died. Its design has very specific religious significance. The five towers that adorn the top layer of the temple represent the five peaks of Mount Meru, home of the Hindu gods, while the moat around it symbolizes the oceans that Hindus believe encircle the world.

The temple of Angkor Wat. The towers represent the peaks of the legendary Mount Meru.

China through the mountains and into the broad valleys of Khmer. In 1432 the Thai destroyed Angkor Wat. The Khmer nobility fled southward and settled near the old Funanese capital (modern Phnom Penh), but Angkor's days of glory were over.

THAIS AND BURMANS

The Thai established the kingdom of Sukhothai under Ramathibodi I in 1351. As they expanded, they came into contact with the people of Burma to the west. The Burmans had migrated from Tibet in the seventh century, subdued smaller tribes, and by the 11th century had founded a powerful state with a large capital city, Pagan. As shepherds, farmers, and merchants, they spread down the Malaysian Peninsula and prospered until the Mongols attacked. Their weakened condition allowed the Thai to move further into Burmese

territory, and for the next 400 years the Thai were the dominant force on the Southeast Asian mainland.

For most of the Middle Ages the eastern side of the mainland peninsula was heavily influenced by China. The area that today makes up northern Vietnam became a Chinese province in the second century B.C. Apart from one brief period, it remained under Chinese control for over 1,000 years and was known first as Nam Viet and later as Annam.

Annam became independent in 939, when it became known as the Dai Co Viet, or the Great Viet State. In a prosperous era the Vietnamese maintained good relations with the new Sung dynasty of China and established their first university in 1076. The Vietnamese then conquered Champa, the enemy kingdom to the south that at one point had occupied the Dai Viet capital at Hanoi. Later, in the late 13th century the Mongols attacked, but a Vietnamese hero named Tran Hung Dao successfully repelled the invasion. In the early 15th century Vietnam was again subject to China, but only briefly—in 1428 the country became independent once again.

ISLAND STATES

The islands that lay to the south of the mainland peninsula were also home to important states. One was the Mataram kingdom of eastern Java, ruled by the Shailendra dynasty. Javanese merchants traded extensively with India, resulting in the islanders adopting the Hindu religion. At the peak of its power, in the early ninth century, Mataram attacked the politically unstable mainland. This assault was a key event in the history of the Khmer Empire, since it forced the Khmer peoples to unite against the intruders. Mataram was defeated, and the Khmer went on to dominate the mainland.

By this time the Shailendra rulers had adopted Buddhism. They were famous for building spectacular temples, the greatest of which was at Borobudur. Erected between 778 and about 850, it is the largest human construction in the Southern Hemisphere. Three miles of winding paths and stairways lead up through towers, shrines, and sculptures. Carvings on the walls depict the road to enlightenment according to Mahayana Buddhism. When Shailendra power declined, the temple was abandoned. It became covered with vegetation and was only rediscovered in the 19th century.

Another important early medieval island state was Srivijaya, located on Sumatra. The state rose to prominence in the seventh century.

Much of Srivijaya's power came from the fact that it controlled the Strait of Malacca. The strait runs between Sumatra and the Malaysian Peninsula, connecting the Indian Ocean to the South China Sea. Whoever controlled the state also controlled all maritime trade between India and China.

Srivijaya's stranglehold on trade eventually led to its downfall. Desperate to gain control of the trade route, the Indian king Rajendra I (1014–1044) attacked Sumatra in 1025, taking the Srivijayan capital Palembang and carrying off many of its treasures. Srivijaya recovered, but never to its former strength.

This statue of Buddha is on the upper terraces of the Buddhist monument Borobudur in Java.

SEE ALSO

- ♦ Architecture
- ♦ China
- ♦ India
- ♦ Mongols
- ♦ Trade

SPANISH KINGDOMS

During the Middle Ages the Iberian Peninsula—modern Spain and Portugal—was made up of separate kingdoms and counties. Muslim armies conquered most of the peninsula in the eighth century. It took centuries for the Christian kingdoms to unite and begin reconquering territory. The last Muslim stronghold—Granada—finally fell in 1492.

At the beginning of the Middle Ages a Germanic tribe, the Visigoths, controlled much of the Iberian Peninsula. By the sixth century they had conquered almost the entire peninsula and made the central city of Toledo their capital. The Visigoths were Arian Christians, who were considered to be heretics, or wrong believers, by the Roman Catholic church. In 587 King Recared (ruled 586–601) decided to become a Roman Catholic.

During the late seventh century the Visigoth nobles warred among themselves as well as rebelling against the monarchy. According to legend, the last Visigothic king, Roderick, raped the daughter of one of his noble counts. The count asked the Muslim peoples of northern Africa to help

The Alcázar in Segovia as it is today. It was the fortified palace of the kings of Castile from the 12th century.

his family gain revenge. On July 19, 711, General Tariq ibn Ziyad sailed across the strait from Morocco with his army and defeated Roderick. The rocky headland on which the Muslims landed was named Gebel (meaning Mount) Tariq after their general, and this name became Gibraltar.

ANDALUSIA
The Muslim armies did not stop there, however. They moved north and by 718 had captured almost the entire peninsula, including the cities of Seville, Toledo, Lisbon, and Valencia. They called their new territory al-Andalus, or Andalusia. By the 10th century it had developed into an independent caliphate (a region ruled by a Muslim leader called a caliph), which was run

The Rock of Gibraltar dominates the 20-mile (32-km) strait between Spain and Morocco. When the Muslim forces invaded Spain in 711, they landed on this headland, naming it Gebel Tariq after their general.

from the capital at Córdoba. The Islamic inhabitants of Andalusia are often called Moors from the Latin *Mauri*, meaning from Mauretania.

The 11th and 12th centuries were a golden age of Moorish culture. Renowned scholars and poets gathered at the Córdoba court, and more than 700 mosques were built. Early in the 11th century, however, internal disagreements led to Andalusia splitting into many small Muslim states. Later, it was reunited under two Muslim dynasties, the Almoravids (1085–1147) and the Almohads (1147–1212). Under Muslim rule Christians formed their own communities within Andalusia. Many learned to speak Arabic and began to adopt elements of Islamic culture. They were known as Mozarabs, meaning "almost Arabs."

Christians outside the borders of Muslim conquest were determined to drive the Muslim forces back to

Africa. In 718, just seven years after the Islamic conquest, a band of Christians, led by a Visigothic nobleman named Pelayo, defeated a Muslim army at Covadonga, near the northern coast. Pelayo ruled a small mountainous kingdom called Asturias, which was centered on the city of Oviedo. In later years this victory was seen as the beginning of the Christians' reconquest of Spain from the Muslims.

KINGDOM OF ASTURIAS

The kings of Asturias gradually expanded their borders westward to include Galicia and south to the Douro River. Around 815, during the reign of Alfonso II (ruled 791–842), the tomb of the apostle James (Santiago in Spanish) was supposedly discovered at what became known as Santiago de Compostela in Galicia.

According to legend, after Saint James was beheaded by Herod

This map shows the kingdoms of the Iberian Peninsula in about 1150. The territory controlled by Islamic rulers had been greatly reduced from its maximum extent in the 10th century.

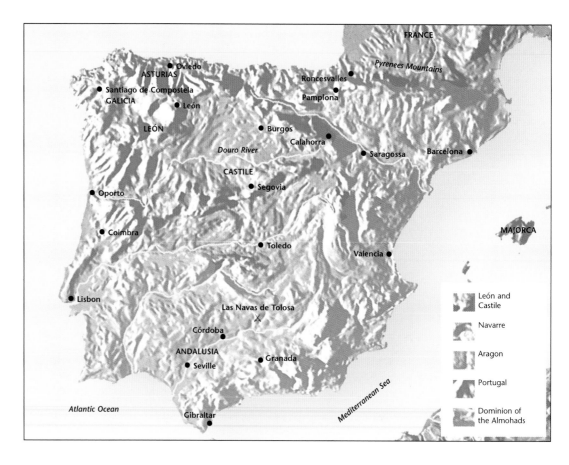

Agrippa in 44 A.D., two of his disciples put his remains in a boat and sailed with them to Galicia. In 815 a shower of shooting stars guided a Galician shepherd to the site of the saint's burial. Alfonso had a basilica built as a monument to Saint James, which included a crypt for the relics of the saint and his two disciples. The Road to Santiago became the most famous of all the pilgrim routes, and Saint James is still the patron saint of modern Spain.

King García I (ruled 910–914) made the city of León his capital. The city had been retaken from the

SANCHO THE GREAT

Sancho III (about 992–1035) was king of Navarre, as well as ruling the neighboring county of Aragon. Like many medieval rulers, Sancho used a combination of marriage, diplomacy, and armed force to extend his influence. In 1029 he added the county of Castile to his realm, having married the daughter of the count of Castile, and the kingdom of León followed five years later. These gains meant that Sancho was able to claim leadership of the whole of Christian Spain, and he was given an imperial crown. He encouraged all Christians to make the pilgrimage to Santiago de Compostela and welcomed the French Benedictine monks of Cluny, who had a great influence throughout Europe. Having brought his dominions together, however, Sancho destroyed his empire by dividing it among his four sons. Each of the sons was given the title of king.

EL CID

Rodrigo Díaz (about 1043–1099) was born in the village of Vivar, near the Castilian city of Burgos. At the age of 22 he was made commander of the Castilian army, and in 1067 he played an important part in a successful campaign against the Islamic kingdom of Saragossa. For his exploits Díaz became known as El Cid, from the Arabic for "lord." In 1081, however, Alfonso VI became convinced that Díaz was plotting against him and had him banished. El Cid gathered together his own small army; and when Christian princes refused his military services, he fought for Saragossa for almost 10 years, before being accepted again by the Castilian king. In 1094 El Cid captured Valencia from the Almoravids after a 20-month siege, and he ruled over the city for the rest of his life. His story was told in a 12th-century epic, or heroic poem, and he later became a Spanish national hero.

El Cid and Martin Gonzalez of Aragon fight to win the city of Calahorra. El Cid won the city for Castile.

Muslims in 850, and the new kingdom of Asturias and León was closely linked to the neighboring county of Castile (the "land of castles") and the independent kingdom of Navarre, which was in the northeast of the peninsula near the Pyrenees Mountains. Navarre's capital was Pamplona, which is famous for its annual fiesta, first held in 1324 and today including a dangerous bull stampede. Navarre reached the height of its power in the 11th century under King Sancho III.

Sancho III died four years after the Muslim kingdom centered on Córdoba had split up. León and Castile soon became a combined kingdom, and their forces moved southward as the Christian reconquest of Spain gained momentum. The town of Segovia was retaken from the Muslims in 1079, and six years later King Alfonso VI of León and Castile captured Toledo.

One of the most important Christian victories over the Muslims was the Battle of Las Navas de Tolosa in 1212. The Castilian king Alfonso VIII led a great army from Castile, Aragon, Navarre, Portugal, and France, routed the Almohads, and brought an end to their power. Encouraged, the Christian kingdoms

PORTUGAL

In 1094 King Alfonso VI of León and Castile rewarded Henry of Burgundy, a French nobleman, for his military help against the Muslims. The king gave Henry the counties of Porto and Coimbra, and named him count of Portugal, after the former Roman city of Porto. The count's son, Alfonso Henriques, considered his inheritance to be a kingdom, and his title of king of Portugal was approved by the pope in 1179. He captured the city of Lisbon from the Muslims in 1147; it became the capital of Portugal in 1256.

Succeeding kings increased the Portuguese crown's power and made further advances against the Muslims. In 1385 Castile tried to take advantage of Portuguese weakness, but John I (the first king of the powerful Aviz dynasty) defeated the Castilian forces and retained the kingdom's independence. One of his sons established a school of navigation and spent his life encouraging voyages of discovery. Known as Henry the Navigator (1394–1460), he was responsible for starting the process that led, after his death, to the Portuguese circumnavigation of Africa and the establishment of Portugal's colonial empire.

The Tower of Belém was built between 1515 and 1521 to guard the mouth of the Tagus River in Lisbon and also to celebrate Portugal's voyages of discovery.

continued their attempts to expel the Muslims. Seville was retaken in 1248, and by the late 13th century the only Muslim territory left was the region around Granada, in the very south.

MUSLIMS AND JEWS

During the 12th and 13th centuries the Christian rulers of the Spanish kingdoms were relatively tolerant of Muslims and Jews. The Muslims (called Mudéjars, from the Arabic for "vassals") preserved their customs and created an architectural style that is famous for its ornamental brickwork and ceramic tiles with elaborate geometric patterns. Jews formed their own communities, and the ruling Christians made separate areas for them within towns. They often worked as tailors and weavers, and a few played an important role as tax collectors. Powerful families emerged within the Jewish communities, and Jewish and Muslim scholars made a great contribution to medieval

Spanish society. Nevertheless, hostility toward Jews grew, and many were forced to convert to Christianity. They were known as *conversos*. Eventually, persecution resulted in widespread massacres toward the end of the 14th century.

UNIFICATION

Throughout the 14th century Castile remained the largest, most powerful Spanish kingdom. However, there were disputes both within the monarchy and with the Castilian nobles, who were always seeking more power. There was also constant friction with Aragon, the second largest and neighboring kingdom. The two kingdoms at last came together in 1479—by marriage. Ten years earlier Princess Isabella of Castile (1451–1504) had married Prince Ferdinand of Aragon

(1452–1516). When they succeeded to the thrones of their respective kingdoms, most of modern Spain came under their joint control.

Ferdinand and Isabella viewed Muslims, Jews, and Christian heretics as a threat to their goal of a united Spain. In 1478 they obtained permission from Pope Sixtus IV (pope 1471–1484) to set up the Inquisition. It dealt severely with heretics, and in 1492 Jews who would not convert to Christianity were driven from the country. That same year Christian forces conquered the last Muslim stronghold of Granada. Twenty years later Ferdinand's troops occupied the small kingdom of Navarre, and the union of Spain was finally complete. The long campaign to recapture Spain from the Muslims is called the Reconquista, which is Spanish for reconquest.

SEE ALSO

♦ Cluny
♦ Exploration
♦ Granada
♦ Heresy
♦ Inquisition
♦ Islamic Empire
♦ Jews and Judaism
♦ Literature
♦ Mediterranean
♦ Pilgrimage

This colored woodcarving of Ferdinand of Aragon and Isabella of Castile dates from the 17th century.

A 14th-century illustration of men practicing archery. Archers made up an important part of medieval armies, and practice was encouraged by kings.

SPORTS AND GAMES

Sports and games have always been important parts of children's play and adults' recreation. In the Middle Ages some sports arose from military skills, such as archery and fencing, while others were for pure entertainment, many being early forms of games played today. They included horseracing, football, tennis, and board games.

Many medieval sports grew out of the skills needed by soldiers. They included the great jousts and tournaments in which knights displayed their horsemanship and fighting skills, and archery, one of the first sports for which records were set: A 13th-century Turkish inscription credits Sultan Mahmud Khan with a shot of 1,215 arrow lengths.

The Turks used powerful bows made of wood and animal horn. The Mongols were also skillful bowmen, who brought their techniques and traditions with them when they invaded Central Asia. In Europe the crossbow—a horizontal bow mounted on a shaft and fired by a trigger—had become a popular weapon by the 12th century, although from the 14th century English archers favored longbows—large wooden bows that were as tall as a man.

In England from the 13th century kings required men aged between 16 and 60 years old to be available to fight for 40 days each year. The kings made bows and arrows available, and encouraged archery practice, banning other sports if they threatened to interfere with practice.

Archery matches were organized between different towns and were often great social occasions. Peasants gathered to watch and often took part in running, jumping, and wrestling contests that were arranged alongside the main event.

SWORDPLAY
Although swordsmanship was also important, most medieval swords were very heavy and did not lend themselves to sporting contest. When gunpowder was introduced in the 14th century, however, defensive

SPLITTING THE WAND

Competing archers shot at small targets from a considerable distance, and the most popular target was a narrow stick, called a wand, that was attached to a target or stuck in the ground. The wand was about an inch (2.5cm) across. According to legend, the English outlaw Robin Hood was an expert archer. In one story Robin and the miller's son Much come upon an archery contest in a forest clearing. Will Scarlet and his band of men are trying to "split the wand" from a distance of 100 yards (90m). None has succeeded; and when Robin asks if he can try, they are amazed when he hits the target three times in a row. Never having seen such bowmanship, and feeling that he has met his master, Scarlet immediately asks Robin Hood to become the leader of his group of outlaws.

armor was used less, and lighter swords were introduced. Guilds, or associations, of fencing masters sprang up throughout Europe. The most famous was the association of St. Marcus of Löwenberg in Germany, which was approved by Holy Roman Emperor Frederick III in 1480. Associations developed and practiced their own secret moves and strokes, which they used to surprise their opponents. Early moves were often rough, incorporating wrestling tricks.

SOCCER AND BALL GAMES

No one knows exactly when the first goal was scored, but ball-kicking games existed in ancient China and Greece. By the seventh century A.D. the Japanese were playing a form of soccer, probably using a ball stuffed with hair. In medieval Europe whole villages challenged each other to rowdy mob games in which a pig's bladder filled with dried peas was kicked toward the opponents' village or goal. In England—where it was

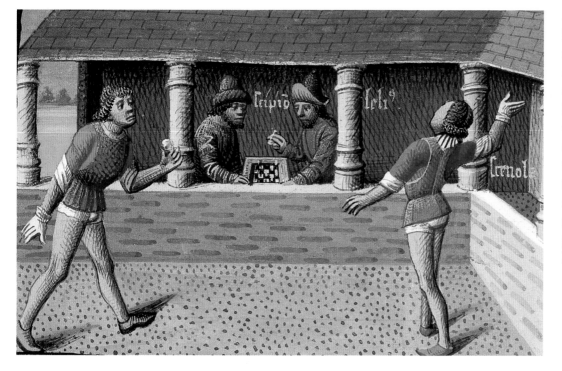

A 15th-century illustration of men playing *jeu de la paume*, an early type of handball from which tennis developed. In the background two men play chess, which was a popular board game in the Middle Ages.

known as "camp-ball"—the game was particularly rough. In 1320 the mayor of London tried to stop the game, and the 14th-century kings Edward III and Richard II officially banned it because it stopped young men from practicing their archery.

In Italy young men played a similar game called *calcio*, which means "kick-ball." The game is still played according to the original rules—or lack of them—in June each year at a festival in Florence. Teams of 27 players represent four different districts of the city and compete for the prize of a live cow, accompanied by much cheering from rival supporters. The modern game of soccer is also called *calcio* in Italy.

Many other ball sports originated in the Middle Ages. Various forms of bowls, in which a ball was thrown or rolled toward a target, were played. In

a game called "stoolball" women sat on milking stools and tried to avoid being hit by a ball thrown by men, who played for prizes of cakes or sometimes kisses. There was also an early form of field hockey, using bent sticks and a large leather ball. A game called "bittle-battle" is mentioned in the Domesday Book, the survey of England made for William the Conqueror in 1086. It was a game played with a stick with a head attached and may have been an early form of golf—which was known in Scotland by the 1450s.

TENNIS

Different forms of handball were played, and in 1427 King James I of Scotland supposedly had a window blocked up because it interfered with his game. So-called real or royal tennis—similar to modern tennis but

WRESTLING

Wrestling was a popular sport in ancient Greece and was practiced in different forms, each with slightly different rules, throughout the medieval world. In western Europe knights of the Holy Roman Empire were taught wrestling as part of their training, while in the Islamic Empire a style of wrestling called *koresh*, introduced by the Turkic peoples, became popular. Sumo, one of the best-known styles of wrestling, developed in Japan in the early Middle Ages. Two wrestlers stood inside a circle and tried to bring their opponent to the ground or to push them out of the circle. Soon many elaborate rituals were attached to sumo wrestling, and it is still practiced today.

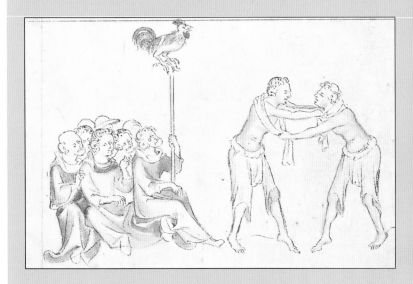

A 14th-century illustration of a wrestling match. Each wrestler grips the other by his clothing in an attempt to make him fall.

played in a walled court off which players can bounce the ball—came originally from the French game known as *jeu de la paume*, or "game of the palm," in which the ball was hit with the hand. This may originally have been a form of handball that was played by churchmen in the cloisters of their monasteries. The oldest surviving tennis court is at Hampton Court, near London, where Henry VIII played in the 1520s.

ANIMAL SPORTS
In the Middle Ages animal fights were considered sport, and people often placed bets on the outcome. Cock-fighting was the most popular form and was known all over the world. In Europe it became traditional for boys to watch fighting cocks or to chase and throw stones at cocks on Shrove Tuesday. These activities were as much part of children's games as spinning tops and blindman's buff.

Bear-baiting was another popular entertainment. The bear was chained to a stake, and dogs were encouraged to attack it. People bet on how many dogs a bear could kill before itself being killed. Baiting also took place with other animals, especially bulls, badgers, and rats. In various parts of the world different animals were set on each other: elephants in India, poisonous spiders in Africa, and even fish in China.

Horses were used for racing. In 12th-century London a horse market was held each Saturday; and to show the speed and power of the horses, boys rode them in competition. This became a form of entertainment to those who watched. The most famous medieval horserace took place in the Italian city of Siena. It is called the Palio after the decorated banner awarded to the winner. The first recorded Palio took place in 1238, and the race is still run today.

A 14th-century illustration of bear-baiting. The bear is chained to a stake by its head, while dogs attack it. Bear-baiting was a popular spectacle in Europe from the 12th to the 19th centuries, after which it was banned as inhumane.

CHILDREN'S GAMES

Medieval children played games that are still familiar today, such as hiding, chasing, and fighting, and children from noble families had similar toys, including dolls and model soldiers and buildings. They played with pets such as dogs, tame squirrels, and birds, but not with cats, which were associated with witches. As they became older, they learned board games, and boys practiced archery, fencing, and hawking.

The origins of chess are obscure, but the game was certainly played in India by the seventh century and in China soon afterward. It arrived in Europe via Persia and the Byzantine Empire by the 10th century, and the Vikings carried the game to England and as far as Iceland. It was a favorite of Henry I of England (ruled 1100–1135) and Alfonso X of Castile (ruled 1252–1284). The simpler game of drafts, also called checkers, was developed in 12th-century France. A chess set was a sign of learning and knowledge, and the game became part of the education of noble boys and girls. In the early 14th century a French Dominican friar even wrote a treatise on chess, which was translated and published a century later by the English printer William Caxton.

Games played with dice were also very popular throughout the Middle Ages, as they had been since ancient times. Playing cards were introduced around the 13th century, although they did not become widespread until printing made it possible to produce identical backs.

BOARD GAMES

A medieval game known as "tables" was an early form of backgammon. Another game called "merrills" had nine pieces for each of the two players and came to be known as "nine men's morris." A more complex form called "fox and geese" was played in 15th-century England by King Edward IV. In northern Europe the Vikings played a game called *hnefatafl*, in which one player tried to protect his king from attack by the opponent's pieces. This northern European game was similar to chess.

SEE ALSO

♦ Arms and Armor
♦ Daily Life
♦ Festivals
♦ Horses
♦ Hunting and Falconry
♦ Italy
♦ Tournaments and Jousts

The Lewis chess set was found on the Isle of Lewis in the Outer Hebrides of Scotland in 1831. The set was made by the Vikings in about the 13th century from carved walrus tusk.

SWITZERLAND

Located in the south of central Europe, and straddling the trade routes running through the Alps between France, Germany, and Italy, Switzerland was a tempting target for outside powers. For much of its history it has had to fight against more powerful neighbors that wanted to control its lands. Victory against the Austrian emperor in 1499 ensured its independence and laid the foundations for modern Switzerland.

Switzerland's history has been shaped by its geography. Two-thirds of its frontiers are formed by high mountain ridges, and its position gave it control of the vital trans-Alpine passes.

The area that became modern Switzerland was originally settled by Celtic and Rhaetian tribes. By the sixth century it had come under the control of the Franks. Later it became part of Charlemagne's Holy Roman Empire. By 1000 it was divided into 12 bishoprics. By the beginning of the 13th century it was made up of semiindependent states called cantons, each ruled by a powerful family.

By the second half of the 13th century the three mountainous central cantons—Unterwalden, Uri, and Schwyz—were being threatened by the Hapsburgs of Austria, who wanted to control the trade route through the St. Gotthard Pass. To combat this threat, the three cantons agreed on a mutual defense pact in 1291. The Hapsburgs went to war to press their claim, but were defeated at the Battle of Morgarten in 1315.

This temporarily thwarted Hapsburg ambitions, and the Swiss embarked on a series of wars over the next 150 years to expand their territory and remove external influence. Other cantons joined the original three; and although the members were occasionally violently divided, they proved sufficiently united to block renewed Hapsburg

SWISS INFANTRY

The Swiss became masters of specialized infantry fighting. Armed with 7-foot (2-m) halberds (a combination of spear, ax, and hook), they formed massed columns when attacking or porcupine formations called *shiltrons* when being attacked. In the 15th century 10 to 20-foot (3 to 6-m) pikes began to replace halberds, although most armies combined the two. The Swiss soon showed that an unarmored man with a halberd or pike was able to kill a heavily armed, armored soldier on foot or on horseback. The Swiss were extremely well-disciplined, an essential quality for successful fighting with halberds and pikes, and soon earned a fearsome reputation. In the 15th and 16th centuries Swiss soldiers were popular mercenaries (paid soldiers) in many European armies.

This 19th-century image depicts the Battle of Granson in 1476. The Swiss decisively defeated the Burgundian army. They lost about 1,000 men, the Swiss only 200.

territorial ambitions at the battles of Sempach in 1386 and Näfels in 1388. A truce was agreed that gave the Swiss a measure of independence, but within the Holy Roman Empire.

However, the Swiss still faced several threats—from the Italian states of Savoy and Milan to the south and the Burgundians to the northeast. War with Savoy between 1403 and 1416 left the Swiss victorious and in control of the Alpine passes into Italy. A war with Milan (1422–1426) was less successful, but the Swiss reached an agreement with their neighbor.

INDEPENDENCE

Conflict with the Hapsburgs, who were backed by the French, ended with a Swiss defeat in 1444 at St. Jakob, but French-Hapsburg losses were so severe that their plans were thrown into disorder. The battle confirmed Switzerland's reputation for having the best, most ferocious soldiers in Europe. The Swiss force of 1,500 men was annihilated, but the 30,000-strong French force lost 3,000 killed and many more wounded. In the late 15th century the Swiss defeated the Burgundians. In 1499 they were victorious against Emperor Maximilian of Austria. He was forced to agree to the Treaty of Basel, which effectively guaranteed Switzerland's independence.

Although the fiercely independent cantons were able to unite when fighting to preserve their homeland and were invariably successful, they found it difficult to agree on national policy, and their attempts to launch attacks were often muddled and unsuccessful. Consequently, the Swiss tended to avoid wars beyond their borders. Slowly, they gained a reputation for neutrality, which continues to this day.

TAMERLANE

The last of the great Mongol leaders, Tamerlane (1336–1405) conquered lands stretching from Russia to the Mediterranean to India, establishing a dynasty that lasted until the early 16th century.

Timur Leng was born in Transoxania (now Uzbekistan) in 1336. As a young man he injured his leg in a riding accident. The injury proved permanent, and he gained the nickname Timur the Lame, or Tamerlane. In 1361 Tamerlane became chieftain of his tribe. He quickly crushed his local rivals and by around 1366 had conquered Transoxania. By this time the Mongol Empire created by Genghis Khan (about 1162–1227) was in decline, crippled by internal feuding. Tamerlane pledged himself to restoring its power and unity.

RISE TO POWER
For the next decade Tamerlane successfully fought rival Mongol rulers for absolute control and embarked on wars to spread or reassert Mongol influence. Between 1383 and 1385 he conquered Persia and then pushed into what are now Iraq and Russia. Next Tamerlane turned east, invading India in 1398. After winning a decisive battle at Panipat in December, he destroyed Delhi and returned to his own capital laden with booty. Much of it was used to turn Samarkand into the most beautiful city in Central Asia.

The following year Tamerlane again turned west and attacked the Mamluks of Syria and Egypt, and the Ottomans of Turkey. In 1401 he occupied Damascus, later attacking Baghdad. Baghdad's capture was followed by the slaughter of some 20,000 of its inhabitants. Next Tamerlane invaded Turkey. He won a great victory over the Ottomans near Ankara in 1402. His final campaign was directed toward China. It began in 1404, but he died in February 1405 before it could be completed. Tamerlane's descendants ruled parts of Central Asia until the early 16th century.

Tamerlane, as shown in a 14th-century Persian illustration.

SEE ALSO
♦ China
♦ Damascus
♦ India
♦ Mamluks
♦ Mongols
♦ Ottoman Empire
♦ Persia
♦ Russia
♦ Warfare

TAXATION AND TITHES

Taxes are sums of money that people have to pay the government, and tithes are a percentage of their produce or income that they are obliged to give the church. In the 13th century, as governments in western Europe became more centralized and the economy more money-based, taxes on income, property, households, and consumer goods became common. Sometimes people thought that taxes were unfair; and when they rose in times of war in the 14th century, they caused popular riots.

A Tax Collector and His Wife (1540) by the 16th-century painter Marinus Claes van Roymerswaele. Tax collectors were unpopular during the Middle Ages, as they were in later times, and here the tax collector is portrayed as a lean, miserly man counting the money he has collected.

In the early Middle Ages there were no restrictions on the dues that kings, nobles, and landowners could impose on their servants. These dues took the form of payments in kind—such as labor and agricultural produce—and money, which became increasingly important in the late Middle Ages. Dues were an effective way of limiting peasants' freedom. For example, it was common for the lord to own the only mill in the village, and peasants had to pay a mill tax—*molitura*—if they wanted to grind their grain there. Lords could tax peasants when they inherited their father's land or married someone from another village.

Landowners also raised income by charging tolls, which were fees for crossing private land or using private bridges, roads, or inland waterways. Merchants attending trade fairs also had to pay market tolls.

TITHES

From the ninth century the church began to impose its own taxes, called tithes. Church tithes amounted to a tenth of the annual proceeds of agriculture and trade, and all Christians had to pay them.

Large barns called tithe barns were built throughout the countryside to store agricultural produce collected in this way. These distinctive buildings can still be seen in Europe today. In many rural areas the local priest was entirely dependent on this form of taxation for his livelihood.

A toll bridge shown in a 15th-century window.

DIRECT TAXATION

By the 13th century the rising costs of government, which now consisted of salaried civil servants, as well as the high costs of war, meant that a more comprehensive taxation system was required. Direct taxation was developed to answer this need. It was a tax based on the value of an individual's movable goods or income from land and movable property such as livestock, gold and silver plate, and jewelry.

Direct taxation was first explored during the Crusades in the late 12th century. By the end of the 13th century it had become widespread, reflecting the increasing powers of centralized governments in Europe.

TAX IN ENGLAND

In 12th-century England direct taxation accounted for only 13 percent of the government's income, and the king was still dependent to a

TAX IN MEDIEVAL CHINA

In eighth-century China, as the government became more efficient, a series of tax reforms transformed the way in which income was generated. Originally, a uniform head tax was raised from the rural population. However, in the eighth century it was replaced with a household tax—based on the value of people's property, including people who lived in towns—and a land tax based on the amount of land people owned and its productivity. In addition to these direct taxes the state generated income in other ways. It controlled the production and sale of important goods, such as salt, alcohol, and tea. Sales taxes were raised from the goods produced by these state monopolies. By 780 the salt monopoly alone produced half the state's total income. Merchants became the government's authorized agents and collected commercial taxes. These taxes grew increasingly lucrative and became more important than direct taxes on small farmers. The tendency to rely on commercial taxation became even more marked during the Sung dynasty (960–1279).

TAX RIOTS

In 1379 oppressive taxes were the main cause of widespread uprisings in Flanders, Paris, and Languedoc in the south of France. In the textile city of Ghent the ruling count imposed a tax on the citizens to pay for a tournament. This obvious abuse of power provoked outrage, and the citizens refused to pay. In Languedoc, falling population levels, caused by the Black Death and the famines of the early 14th century, meant that the hearth tax was becoming less lucrative. In response, it was raised, and tax collectors were empowered to enter and search houses. Outraged citizens refused to pay the new taxes, and riots broke out. In 1382 new sales taxes were imposed on wine, salt, and other merchandise. Shopkeepers locked out tax-collectors, who were instructed to assess taxable merchandise. In Rouen protesters against these oppressive taxes ran riot. They rampaged through the houses of the rich and, drunk on stolen wine, killed royal officials and tax collectors. The local abbey, notorious for its land-holdings and tax privileges, was attacked by an enraged mob.

A 19th-century print showing rampaging tax rioters in the French capital of Paris in 1382.

large extent on the profits he made as a landowner. Direct taxation began to be used in the 13th century. In 1207 tax was set at a rate of one-thirteenth of the value of people's movable goods, which produced a substantial income for the Crown.

Customs duties—taxes imposed on imported, or less commonly exported, goods—were also an important source of income. They were raised on valuable goods such as wool, wine, and cloth. In 1275 the wool tax became permanent and between 1275 and 1294 raised £8,000 to £13,000 a year. From 1217 the pope required the church to subsidize the king, especially if he was actively engaged in the Crusades.

The king could only raise taxes with the consent of the church, merchants, and people. This need for consultation and approval stimulated the growth of parliament—it was important that there was a forum in which subjects could debate the king's financial requirements and approve any moves to raise direct taxes.

Extraordinary taxes raised in times of war could nevertheless provoke strong feelings. In 1381 a head tax —a tax of a uniform amount payable

A 15th-century illustration of the Mongol emperor Kublai Khan's tax collectors receiving and recording taxes from merchants. The picture comes from a copy of the book written by the Italian merchant Marco Polo (1254–1324) about his travels in the east.

by everyone—was raised to finance England's conflict with France. When villagers in Kent and Essex refused to pay, the Peasants' Revolt began, as the villagers marched on London and demanded the abolition of the tax.

TAX IN FRANCE

In France taxation caused social unrest. Direct taxation was imposed through a combination of hearth taxes—a tax on each household—and sales taxes. The tax on the sale of salt, called the *gabelle*, was particularly unpopular. Nobles and the clergy were exempt from taxation. The basic assumption behind French taxation policy was that the payment of taxes was ignoble: Knights did not pay because they served the state with their swords, not with their purses. The result was an unjust system in which the poor were taxed far more heavily than the rich.

It was assumed in France that, under normal circumstances, the king should be able to live off his own estates and should only have recourse to raising taxes during times of conflict or crisis. In 1355 King John applied to the Estates-General—the national assembly of representatives from the three groups, or estates, of French society—for taxes to pay for his troops.

The Estates agreed to support 30,000 soldiers for a year and proposed to raise the money by an income tax. The wealthiest were expected to pay a tax of 4 percent on their income, while the lowest taxable class were to pay a tax of 10 percent. This unjust division of the tax burden, which provoked a revolt among the textile-workers of Arras, was the beginning of a series of tax revolts that led to civil unrest in the latter part of the 14th century.

SEE ALSO

♦ Architecture
♦ Charity
♦ Church
♦ Feudalism
♦ Government
♦ Money
♦ Parliaments
♦ Peasant Uprisings
♦ Property and Land

TEUTONIC KNIGHTS

The Teutonic Knights began as a charitable order in Palestine (modern Israel) in 1189. They became one of the most prominent and victorious military orders in Europe, dominating Prussia and the Baltic coast. After they lost the Battle of Tannenberg in 1410, their power steadily diminished. In 1839 they became a charitable order again, and today their headquarters are in Vienna, Austria.

The history of the Teutonic Knights began when German merchants set up a house in Jerusalem to look after pilgrims in 1189. In 1198 they became a military order of knight-monks. Like the other military orders, their purpose was to provide military support to the Crusader states. Members had to be German, of legitimate birth, and from a knightly family.

In 1226 Duke Conrad of Mazovia (in modern Poland) invited the Teutonic Knights to help him fight the pagan Prussian tribes threatening his northwestern borders. The grand master of the order, Hermann von Salza, negotiated charters from Emperor Frederick II and Pope Gregory IX, granting the order in advance absolute title to all the territory they might conquer.

The "Northern Crusade" began in 1233 using volunteers recruited from Germany. The conquest of Prussia took 50 years to complete and was extremely brutal. Because they were fighting pagans, the knights took no prisoners and also killed women and children. The Prussians outnumbered the knights, but they did not have the organization or equipment necessary to besiege the hundreds of well-defended stone fortresses the knights built as bases for their raids. When the knights had successfully depopulated an area, they imported peasants from Germany and founded new Christian settlements.

By 1283 the Prussians had virtually been wiped out; the few who survived were forced to become Christians. Prussia became an independent state ruled by the Teutonic Knights. In

The knights' massive fortress at Marienburg (Malbork) in modern Poland as it is today. From the 13th to the 15th century it was one of the most powerful fortresses in Europe. It has been extended and restored.

LITHUANIAN CAMPAIGN

Between 1309 and 1410 the Teutonic Knights campaigned relentlessly against Lithuania. The prestige of the order was high, and the knights promoted their campaign as a kind of military college, where young noblemen and knights and their soldiers from all over northern Europe could gain experience in real warfare in a crusade. Those who fought successfully against the pagans were rewarded with a place at Marienburg's "Table of Honor." Although Lithuania became Christian after 1386, the knights continued to raid it.

The border between Lithuania and Prussia had natural defenses of trackless forest mixed with bogland. The climate meant that there were only two opportunities in the year for raiding: about two months during the winter, when it was cold enough for the surface of the bogs to freeze over but not yet cold enough to kill the foot soldiers; and about one month in the summer, when sun and wind made the bogs dry enough to cross. Either "window" could be destroyed by a summer rainstorm or a sudden thaw.

1291 the knights left Palestine, and in 1309 the grand master built a magnificent residence for the order's headquarters at Marienburg. The knights now concentrated on the pagan Lithuanians (see box).

In 1386 Grand Duke Jagiello of Lithuania converted to Christianity in order to marry Queen Jadwiga of Poland. Under his Christian name of Wladyslaw II he set about converting his people. The knights, however, continued to raid Lithuania. By this time they had control over a very large territory, including trading centers on the Baltic coast. They were also extremely rich because the pope had released them from their vows of poverty in 1263 and permitted them to engage in trading and banking.

DEFEAT AT TANNENBERG

In 1408 a rebellion broke out in Samogitia; it attracted all those who held grudges against the knights. Wladyslaw II and his Polish army joined forces with the Lithuanians, Samogitians, and various others. The knights suffered a crushing defeat at the Battle of Tannenberg in 1410.

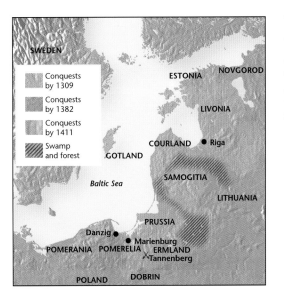

This map shows the territories conquered by the Teutonic Knights between 1233 and 1410.

The grand master and hundreds of knights and foot soldiers were killed. The defeat permanently damaged the order's military power and authority. The knights were forced to cede Samogitia, Pomerelia, land along both banks of the Vistula River, and Ermland to Poland after the Thirteen Years' War (1454–1466). They kept control of Prussia, but only as a fief of Poland, for which the grand master had to do homage to the Polish king. The wholly German order was also forced to accept Polish members.

SEE ALSO

♦ Baltic States
♦ Crusader States
♦ Crusades
♦ Poland

TEXTILES

Textiles were important during the Middle Ages not only for making clothes and furnishings, but also as signs of power and wealth. They ranged from coarse woolen clothes made by peasants for their own use to fabulous silks with intricate designs produced in workshops attached to royal courts. Cloth trading was important throughout the Middle Ages, and by the end of the period the manufacture of woolen cloth had become the biggest industry in western Europe.

The term textile is usually applied to woven cloth, but it can also be used to describe fabrics made using other methods. Since ancient times weaving has been the most widespread way of making cloth. It is a technique based on two sets of parallel threads: the warp, which runs longways, and the weft, which is threaded through it. The warp threads are held tight on frames called looms, which became more efficient during the Middle Ages.

Another method of making textiles in the Middle Ages was felting. It was a simple process that involved soaking wool in water and scrubbing and pressing it so that the fibers matted together. Felted cloth was very warm and was widely used for blankets, rugs, cloaks, and large tents, called yurts, in Central Asia and the Middle East.

Knitting was also used to make clothes. Because it was more time-consuming than weaving and produced smaller pieces of cloth, it was used for domestic rather than commercial production.

A 14th-century illustration of a woman weaving on a loom. Her feet operate a device called a treadle that lifts one set of the warp threads so that the weft thread can be run beneath them.

DIFFERENT FIBERS
In western Europe almost all textiles were made from wool in the Middle Ages, and by 1300 the production of woolen cloth had become the region's largest manufacturing industry. The finest wool came from England, and weaving was concentrated in the Low Countries—modern Belgium and the Netherlands; a little later northern Italy also became an important center.

However, the most sought-after and precious fiber was silk, which is made from the cocoons of silk-moth caterpillars. The ancient Chinese were the first to discover how to make silk and kept it a closely guarded secret. However, by 1000 B.C. Chinese merchants began to trade silk abroad, along routes that became known as

Modern Mongolians applying a thick layer of felt to the outside of a large tent, called a yurt. They use materials that have changed little since the Middle Ages.

silk roads. Countries along these routes, such as India and Persia, also became important centers of silk production. In the sixth century a flourishing silk industry grew up around the Byzantine court in Constantinople, when Emperor Justinian I (ruled 527–565) persuaded two Persian monks who had lived in China to return there and smuggle out some silkworms. However, countries in western Europe did not discover how to make silk until the 14th century, when Italy became a major center for the production of silk textiles.

DYEING

Textiles were colored using natural dyes that were obtained from plants and sometimes from animals and minerals. Most red dyes came from plants belonging to the madder family, which could be grown practically anywhere, and a red that had been highly valued from ancient times was made from the cochineal beetle. Yellow dyes came from plants such as crocuses—saffron is made from their stamens—and turmeric. Blues were obtained from indigo, which was cultivated in India and widely exported, and from woad, a plant common in Europe and the Near East. Many other local plants were also used. Some dyes were rare and extremely expensive, and because of this became signs of wealth and status. One of them was "royal purple," a dye made from a shellfish called murex. It had first been manufactured by the ancient Phoenicians and was later used for the robes of Roman emperors. It was still much treasured in the Middle Ages, and laws were passed restricting its use to royalty. For example, the Byzantine emperors issued legislation between the fourth and sixth centuries that permitted only imperial silk factories to use the dye.

Cotton, which comes from a plant, originated in India and parts of Africa. It was widely used in these hot countries as well as those of the Islamic Empire and the eastern Mediterranean during the Middle Ages, but was not introduced to western Europe until the 14th century. Another plant used to make textiles was flax, from which linen is made. It had been used by the ancient Egyptians and by the time of the Romans was cultivated throughout western Europe.

USES AND VALUE

Textiles had a wide variety of practical uses in the Middle Ages. They were used for clothing; for hangings to cover cold walls and drafty windows and doors; for rugs, blankets, and saddle cloths; and for large tents such as those used by Islamic and Ottoman rulers when they traveled around their territories. They were important in the home, in church, and on the battlefield, where they were used for livery, banners, and battle standards.

They were also items of great value and were used to display wealth. Yarns made from precious metals such as gold and silver were often incorporated into silks and embroidered textiles, increasing their value as well as creating a dazzling effect.

Fine cloth also indicated rank, and rulers often gave special robes to members of the nobility and the royal court. In the east textile factories attached to royal courts flourished as they supplied this demand.

A piece of silk woven in Spain in about the 14th century with gold and silver thread.

The Byzantine court was particularly famous for its lavish silks, which were much admired by rulers in western Europe. Byzantine emperors made gifts of these fabrics to foreign courts and also used them for political ends, offering silks to foreign rulers on favorable terms in return for naval or military support to help defend threatened Byzantine territories.

CLOTH MAKERS

The people who made textiles varied from peasant families who crafted their own basic clothes to large, highly organized workshops, either attached to royal courts or owned and run by merchants. Although both women and men were involved in making textiles for their own families, only men worked in commercial workshops.

In the east workshops of skilled craftsmen making silks had long been attached to courts, such as those of the Sassanids in Persia, the Byzantine emperors in Constantinople, and the Abassids in Islamic lands. Privately run workshops also grew up in the towns and cities there.

In western Europe commercial textile production was largely carried out in people's homes under the supervision of an agent—a system known as cottage industry. Organized workshops in towns, and guilds to regulate them, only began to develop on a wide scale from the 13th century when the wool trade expanded.

THEATER AND ENTERTAINMENT

Dramatic performances in the Middle Ages were almost exclusively religious in character. They began as commentaries performed by priests in church and developed into cycles of plays performed by actors in the streets; they often lasted a whole day or more. Traveling groups of actors, acrobats, clowns, and trained animals also put on performances at markets and fairs, and entertained nobles in their courts.

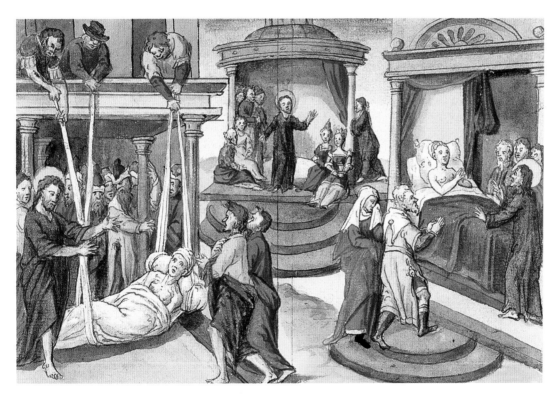

An illustration from about 1500 showing scenes from a mystery play staged in the French town of Valenciennes. At left Christ heals a paralyzed man who has been lowered through the roof to get past the crowd outside; in the middle Christ preaches; and on the right he cures a sick woman.

One of the most popular forms of drama at the end of the Roman Empire was mime, which was different from modern mime, or silent acting. Roman mimes were short performances that dealt with familiar themes and poked fun at well-known public figures. Because they were often rude and irreverent, they soon attracted the displeasure of the Christian church, and in 401 actors were forbidden from taking the sacraments.

Condemned in this way and lacking official support, performers became itinerant, traveling from place to place. They formed groups, or troupes, and dressed in bright colors and outrageous costumes to advertise their performances and attract people to watch them. Their performances consisted of plays with improvised dialogue, stock—or set—characters, songs, dances, and acrobatics.

RELIGIOUS PLAYS

In the Middle Ages the church began to develop its own type of drama in the form of tropes, dramatic commentaries on biblical texts that were performed by priests as part of services. These dramatizations began around the 10th century and were performed in church, sometimes on special sets. They became popular with congregations, but in the 13th century the pope ordered that they be held outside churches, fearing they overshadowed the true meaning of religious ceremonies. Tropes then developed into the three main types of medieval drama: the morality, miracle, and mystery plays.

MEDIEVAL DRAMAS

In morality plays the characters were allegorical (symbolic) representations of good and evil, and the plays' action concerned the struggle between them. One of the best-known morality plays is the 15th-century English play *Everyman*, which treats the theme of death and the fate of the human soul.

Miracle plays reenacted the lives, miracles, or martyrdoms of saints. They were first performed by members of the clergy in Latin and later by secular actors.

Mystery plays were based on biblical subjects and were performed in vernacular, or local, languages—as opposed to Latin—by members of trade guilds. Guilds competed with each other to produce the most lavish sets, props, and costumes for their plays, and performed an appropriate story—for example, boatbuilders would act out the story of Noah.

A 15th-century illustration of a court jester. Jesters, or fools, were popular members of medieval courts, where they entertained the lord and his household. They wore distinctive brightly colored clothes adorned with bells and a hood with ears, and they carried a short staff.

By the 13th century many irreverent details and humorous touches had been added to the original religious stories. Because of this the church ceased to support the plays, which contributed to the end of mystery plays in the 16th century.

Almost every cathedral town in Europe held performances of mystery plays. In time sponsorship by the guilds led to cycles—or series—of as many as 50 plays being performed one after another. These cycles often lasted a whole day or more. Parts of some of these cycles survive and are still performed in a few English cities such as Chester, York, Coventry, and Wakefield.

Some play cycles were presented in one place on a large stage outside the cathedral or in the marketplace. These stages often had sets of heaven and hell at either end and elaborate mechanical devices to portray fire-breathing monsters, flying angels, and gruesome martyrdoms. In England

JAPANESE NOH THEATER

Noh is a traditional form of Japanese theater that developed around the 14th century. It is based on well-known stories that are told with minimal dialogue and rely on the appearance of the performers and their movements for expression. The performers interpret rather than enact the stories, and their skill is central to the art form—"noh" means "talent" or "skill." Plays are usually short and provide a structure for movement and music, which is performed by a small group of musicians and singers. The scenery and props are also minimal.

There are five different types of noh play, their subjects ranging from gods, fighting, and devils to those based on "present-day" themes. Two of the most important noh writers were Kan'ami Kiyotsugu (1333–1384) and his son Zeami Motokiyo (1363–1443). As well as writing many plays, Zeami devised principles that guided noh performers for many centuries. Noh theater remains a popular art form in Japan today.

Modern actors performing a noh play in Kyoto, Japan. They wear traditional costume and use stylized gestures.

most mystery plays were performed on pageant wagons, large, flat-topped carts that were rolled through the streets, stopping at designated stations where the play was acted.

ENTERTAINMENTS

Throughout the Middle Ages actors, musicians, minstrels, dancers, fools, acrobats, jugglers, and trained animals provided entertainments wherever people gathered. They were often part of noble and royal courts—musicians were especially valued—providing lavish spectacles and entertainments.

Markets and fairs were also key settings for traveling entertainers, especially from the 13th century, when they became increasingly social occasions. People gathered to watch performers and trained animals such as bears, monkeys, horses, and dogs putting on shows, although more organized performances known as circuses did not develop until much later, in the 18th century.

Another popular entertainment in the Middle Ages was dancing. The most common medieval dances were the peasant round dances, in which people joined hands or linked arms around a leader and sang popular songs called carols. They were often raucous expressions of joy and passion, accompanied by much singing. A more refined type of dancing was performed in courts. Here the emphasis was on elaborate steps, and dancers were accompanied by musical instruments.

SEE ALSO

- Chaucer, Geoffrey
- Courtly Love
- Dante
- Fairs and Markets
- Festivals
- Guilds
- Literature
- Music
- Sports and Games
- Tournaments and Jousts

THOMAS AQUINAS

Thomas Aquinas (about 1225–1274) was one of the greatest thinkers of the late Middle Ages. He tackled the main intellectual problem of the time—how to reconcile faith with reason—and his answer provided a firm basis for Christian doctrine. In 1323 he was made a saint.

A 15th-century painting of Thomas Aquinas. Many of his ideas were condemned in the Middle Ages but in 1879 his work was made the official philosophy of the Catholic church.

Aquinas was born at Aquino near Naples, Italy, into a noble family. As a teenager, despite the objections of his family, he joined the Dominicans, a teaching order of monks. Because he was large and quiet, his fellow students called him "dumb ox," but his studies at the universities of Naples, Paris, and Cologne revealed his genius. He received a master's degree and taught in Italy, Spain, and Paris.

PHILOSOPHICAL WORKS

Aquinas wrote many commentaries on scripture and on Greek philosophy, but two of his works are especially renowned. *Summa Contra Gentiles* explains Christian doctrine—vital for Dominican missionaries in particular. The *Summa Theologiae* is a systematic presentation of knowledge, with explanations of how it is acquired. He approached over 600 topics by asking questions, then posing and answering 10,000 possible objections.

The problems Aquinas tackled had arisen when works written by the ancient Greek philosopher Aristotle were translated into Latin in the 12th century. Aristotle had taught that all knowledge, or truth, is based on what we experience with our senses and explain with reason. The church, on the other hand, taught that truth comes from God's revelation and is accepted by faith. These two systems seemed to be incompatible.

Aquinas explained reason and faith in such a way that those who adopted Aristotle's system could integrate it with Christianity. He believed that the human mind perceives truth in nature through senses and reason, but supernatural truth by faith. The meeting point between the two hinges on knowledge of the existence of God, which can come through faith or through reason. He argued that many other spiritual truths were also provable through logical reasoning. This meant that reason and faith were compatible. His work provoked great controversy, and after his death some parts were condemned by the church.

SEE ALSO

♦ Religious Thought and Philosophy
♦ Roman Catholic Church
♦ Scholasticism

GLOSSARY

A.D. Anno Domini ("the year of our Lord") was the year that Christ was born. All dates with these letters written after them are measured forward from his birth to the present day.

alms Money, food, or gifts given to the poor.

apprentice Someone legally bound for a period of years to a craftsman in order to learn a craft.

aristocracy A privileged section of society, also called the nobility, whose members attained their position through birth rather than merit.

barbarian A name often given to peoples who did not belong to a particular civilization and were considered to be savage and backward.

B.C. Before Christ All dates with these letters written after them are measured backward from Christ's birth date.

blasphemy Words or actions disrespectful to sacred figures, beliefs, or objects.

bureaucracy A part of government relying on specialized administrators and hierarchies (ranks) of officials; characterized by a large amount of paperwork and many regulations.

Buddhism An Indian religion following the teaching of the Buddha (enlightened one), based on the idea that humans can be freed from suffering by self-purification, known as enlightenment.

caliph An Islamic ruler.

caravan A group of people traveling together with animals to carry their goods.

charter A grant of rights and privileges given by a ruler to an individual, community, or nation.

classical A term referring to the cultures of ancient Greece and Rome.

Crusade A military expedition undertaken by European Christians to capture the Holy Land from the Muslims.

diocese The name of a territory under the control of a bishop.

doctrine A specific principle or belief, or a system of beliefs, taught by the church.

dynasty A series of rulers from the same family.

excommunication A decree issued by the Roman Catholic church that prevents an individual from taking part in any sacraments or rites.

heresy A belief contrary to the accepted teachings and beliefs of a religion.

icon A holy image of a sacred figure or event depicted in a stylized way and used during worship in the Orthodox church.

imam An Islamic leader of prayers at a mosque.

infidel Term used by Christians to describe non-Christians.

Islam The Muslim religion based on the teachings of the Prophet Muhammad as laid out in the holy book of the Koran, the basic principle of which is submission to God.

mercenary A soldier who will fight for any employer in return for wages.

Muslim A follower of Islam.

nomads People who wander from place to place rather than living in a settled community.

patriarch The title given to a few powerful church leaders: the bishops of Antioch, Rome, Alexandria, Constantinople, and Jerusalem.

philosophy A search for truth or wisdom through logical reasoning; also the beliefs of an individual or group.

pilgrimage A long journey made to a sacred place as an act of religious devotion.

sacrament A Christian rite, or ceremony, that is an outward sign of inner faith.

Saracen A name used in the Middle Ages for an Arab or a Muslim.

secular Belonging to the civil rather than the church authorities.

siege A military blockade of a fortress or a city in order to force it to surrender, often by cutting off its supplies of food and water.

theology A field of study devoted to religious faith.

tithe A tax of one-tenth of a person's annual produce or income payable to the local church.

tribute A payment made by a subject or nation in recognition of an overlord's power.

usury The name given to charging interest on a loan, a practice that was considered sinful by the medieval church.

vernacular The native or local language of an area, for example, French in France, as opposed to an official language, such as Latin.

TIMELINE

306 Constantine I becomes emperor of Rome	**711** Muslims begin conquest of Spain	**c. 950** Harold Bluetooth unites Denmark
330 Constantine moves his capital from Rome to Byzantium	**720** Illuminated manuscript of Lindisfarne Gospels produced	**955** German knights defeat Magyars at Battle of Lechfeld
410 Visigoths sack Rome	**726** Venice elects first doge; Byzantine emperor Leo III orders that all icons be destroyed	**960** Sung dynasty gain power in China
c.431 Saint Patrick introduces Christianity to Ireland	**750** Abbasids overthrow Umayyad dynasty	**982** Erik the Red sets out on first expedition to Greenland
434 Attila becomes leader of the Huns	**754** Pope crowns Pippin III as king of the Franks	**987** Hugh Capet becomes king of France, founding Capetian dynasty
451 Coptic church splits from Orthodox church	**778** Construction of Borobudur begins	**988** Vladimir I of Kiev converts to Christianity
452 Attila the Hun invades Italy	**790** Offa's Dyke built to separate England from Wales	
476 Romulus Augustulus, last emperor of western Roman Empire, deposed	**793** Norsemen attack Lindisfarne, England, in one of the first Viking raids	**c. 1000** Leif Eriksson lands on coast of Newfoundland
	794 Emperor Kammu of Japan moves capital to Heian	**1000** Stephen I becomes first king of Hungary
527 Justinian becomes emperor of eastern Roman Empire		**1014** Byzantine emperor Basil II defeats Bulgarians at Serres
529 Saint Benedict establishes monastery at Monte Cassino	**800** Charlemagne crowned emperor of the Romans by pope in Rome	**1016** King Canute of Denmark seizes throne of England
531 Khosrow I begins rule of Sassanid Empire	**c. 802** Jayavarman II unifies Khmer peoples	**c. 1040** Movable-type printing develops in China
581 China unified under the Sui dynasty	**863** Missionaries Cyril and Methodius begin to convert Slavs to Christianity	**1054** Orthodox, or Eastern, church splits from Roman Catholic church
590 Gregory the Great becomes pope	**871** Alfred the Great becomes king of Wessex	**1055** Seljuk Turks take control of Baghdad
618 T'ang dynasty established in China	**882** Oleg makes Kiev capital of Rus	**1066** William the Conqueror defeats Anglo-Saxons at Battle of Hastings
622 Muhammad's flight from Mecca to Medina, later known as the *hegira*	**885** Vikings begin siege of Paris	**1071** Seljuk Turks defeat Byzantines at Battle of Manzikert
	c. 896 Magyars settle in Hungary	
633 Islamic Empire begins to expand across Middle East		**1096** Start of First Crusade
638 Muslims under Umar I occupy Jerusalem	**910** Cluny monastery founded in Burgundy	**1099** City of Jerusalem falls to Crusaders
661 Mu'awiyah makes Damascus capital of the Umayyad Empire	**911** Charles III grants area of land—later called Normandy —to Viking leader Rollo	**c. 1119** Knights Templar established
676 Peninsula of Korea united under kings of Silla	**918** Wang Kon founds kingdom of Koryo	**1130** Roger II crowned king of Sicily
681 First Bulgar state formed	**939** State of Annam becomes independent from China	**1147** Start of Second Crusade
		c. 1150 Gothic style of architecture begins to appear in Europe
705 Construction of Great Mosque of Damascus begins		**1154** Henry II becomes first Plantagenet king of England;

Arab scholar al-Idrisi creates map of known world

1155 Frederick I becomes Holy Roman emperor, the first ruler to hold the title

1158 First university founded at Bologna

1170 Archbishop of Canterbury Thomas Becket is murdered

1171 Saladin becomes sultan of Egypt

1187 Saladin recaptures Jerusalem for Muslims, triggering Third Crusade in 1189

1192 Minamoto Yoritomo becomes shogun of Japan

1204 Crusaders capture Constantinople

1206 Mongol chieftain Temüjin takes the title Genghis Khan, or Universal Ruler; Qutbud-Din founds sultanate of Delhi

1209 Start of Albigensian Crusade; Followers of Saint Francis form the Friars Minor

1215 Magna Carta granted by King John I of England; Pope Innocent III frees Christians from financial debts to Jews; Mongol forces destroy Chinese city of Chengdu

1216 Dominican order founded

1226 Louis IX becomes king of France

1230 Guillaume de Lorris begins to write the *Romance of the Rose*

1231 Pope Gregory IX authorizes inquisition against heretics

1233 Teutonic Knights begin conquest of Prussia

1238 Nasrid dynasty take over kingdom of Granada

1240 Mongols destroy Kiev

1242 Alexander Nevsky defeats Teutonic Knights

1243 Mongols defeat Seljuk Turks at Battle of Kosedagh

1248 Start of Seventh Crusade

1250 Mamluk general Aibak seizes power in Egypt

1252 Pope Innocent IV authorizes use of torture against suspected heretics

1258 Mongols capture Baghdad

1260 Cairo becomes capital of Mamluk Empire; Mamluks defeat Mongols at Battle of Ain Jalut

1271 Marco Polo embarks on journey to court of Kublai Khan

1274 Pope Gregory X recognizes Rudolf I as first Hapsburg Holy Roman emperor

c. 1275 Formation of Hanseatic League

1279 Kublai Khan establishes Yüan dynasty in China

1291 Crusaders finally leave Palestine

1297 William Wallace leads Scottish rebellion against King Edward I of England

1302 Flemish footsoldiers defeat French knights at Battle of Courtrai; First Estates General held in France

1307 Dante begins work on *The Divine Comedy*

1309 Popes move to Avignon

1312 Mansa Musa becomes king of Mali

1314 Robert Bruce defeats Edward II at Bannockburn

1336 Hindu kingdom of Vijayanagara founded in India

1337 Start of Hundred Years' War between England and France

1346 First recorded use of gunpowder weapons in Europe at Battle of Crécy

1347 Black Death arrives in Europe

1368 Mongols lose control of northern China;

Chinese Ming dynasty established

1377 Pope Gregory XI calls for arrest of John Wycliffe for heresy

1378 Beginning of Great Schism

1380 Dmitry Donskoy defeats Mongols at Battle of Kulikovo

1381 Peasants' Revolt breaks out in England

c. 1385 Geoffrey Chaucer begins work on *Canterbury Tales*

1386 Duke Jagiello of Lithuania becomes king of Poland, starting new dynasty

1396 Ottoman sultan Bayezid I defeats crusaders at Battle of Nicopolis

1397 Sweden, Norway, and Denmark are united under Union of Kalmar

1401 Tamerlane sacks Damascus

1410 Teutonic Knights defeated at Battle of Tannenberg

1415 Jan Hus executed for heresy; English forces under Henry V defeat French at Agincourt

1429 Joan of Arc leads French army to victory at Orléans

1453 Constantinople falls to Ottoman Turks under Mehmed II

1455 Start of Wars of the Roses; Invention of Gutenberg system of printing

1462 Ivan the Great becomes grand prince of Moscow

1485 Henry VII becomes first Tudor king of England

1492 Christian forces conquer Granada

1493 Muhammad Askia begins rule of Songhai Empire

1504 Michelangelo completes his marble statue of David

1517 Ottoman sultan Selim I defeats Mamluks to take control of Syria and Egypt

FURTHER READING

BOOKS

Aldred, D.H., *Castles and Cathedrals: The Architecture of Power 1066–1550*. New York: Cambridge University Press, 1993.

Allan, T., *Legends of Chivalry: Medieval Myth*. Alexandria, VA: Time Life Inc., 2000.

Bingham, J., Gower J., and Wood G., *Medieval World*. London, UK: Usborne Publishing Ltd, 1999.

Breuilly, E., O'Brien, J., and Palmer, M., *Religions of the World: The Illustrated Guide to Origins, Beliefs, Traditions, and Festivals*. New York: Checkmark Books, 1997.

Bull, S., *An Historical Guide to Arms and Armor*. New York: Facts on File, 1991.

Corbishley, M., *The Middle Ages: A Cultural Atlas for Young People*. New York: Facts on File, 1990.

Corrain, L., Ricciardi, S., and Ricciardi A., *Giotto and Medieval Art: The Lives and Works of Medieval Artists*. New York: Peter Bedrick Books, 1995.

Gies, F. and J., *Cathedral, Forge, and Waterwheel: Technology and Invention in the Middle Ages*. New York: HarperPerennial Library, 1995.

Gimpel, J., *The Medieval Machine: The Industrial Revolution of the Middle Ages*. New York: Penguin USA, 1977.

Grant, N., *The Vikings*. New York: Oxford University Press, 1998.

Gravett, C., and Dann, F., *Eyewitness: Castle*. New York: DK Publishing, 2000.

Gravett, C., and Dann, F., *Eyewitness: Knight*. New York: DK Publishing, 2000.

Gregory, T., *The Dark Ages*. New York: Facts on File, 1993.

Hanawalt, B.A., *The Middle Ages: An Illustrated History*. New York: Oxford University Press, 1998.

Haywood, J., *The Medieval World (World Atlas of the Past, Volume 2)*. New York: Oxford University Press, 2000.

Hicks, P., *How Castles Were Built*. Austin, TX: Raintree/Steck Vaughn, 1998.

Hicks, P., *Technology in the Time of the Vikings*. Austin, TX: Raintree/Steck Vaughn, 1998.

Hinds, K., *The City (Life in the Middle Ages)*. Tarrytown, NY: Benchmark Books, 2000.

Hinds, K., *The Countryside (Life in the Middle Ages)*. Tarrytown, NY: Benchmark Books, 2000.

Jones, P.M., *Medieval Medicine in Illuminated Manuscripts*. London, UK: British Library Publications, 1999.

Jordan, W.C., *The Middle Ages: A Watts Guide for Children*. Danbury, CT: Franklin Watts Inc., 2000.

Langley, A., *Eyewitness: Medieval Life*. New York: DK Publishing, 2000.

Langley, A., and Dennis, P., *DK Discoveries: Castles at War*. New York: DK Publishing, 2000.

MacDonald, F., *Marco Polo: A Journey through China*. Danbury, CT: Franklin Watts Inc., 1998.

MacDonald, F., *The Middle Ages*. New York: Facts on File, 1993.

MacDonald, F., *The World in the Time of Charlemagne*. Broomall, PA: Chelsea House Publishing, 2000.

MacDonald, F., and Bergin, M., *A Medieval Castle*. New York: Peter Bedrick Books, 1993.

MacDonald, F., and James, J., *A Medieval Cathedral*. New York: Peter Bedrick Books, 1991.

Margeson, S.M., and Anderson, P., *Eyewitness: Viking*. New York: DK Publishing, 2000.

Marshall, C., *Warfare in the Medieval World*. Austin, TX: Raintree/Steck Vaughn, 1998.

Martell, H., *The World of Islam before 1700*. Austin, TX: Raintree/Steck Vaughn, 1998.

McNeill, S., *The Middle Ages*. New York: Oxford University Press, 1998.

Power, E.E., *Medieval Women*. New York: Cambridge University Press, 1997.

Roden, K., *The Plague*. Providence, RI: Copper Beech Books, 1996.

Sheehan, S., *Great African Kingdoms*. Austin, TX: Raintree/Steck Vaughn, 1999.

Shuter, J., *The Middle Ages*. Westport, CT: Heinemann Library, 1999.

Simpson, J., and Michaelson, C., *Ancient China*. Alexandria, VA: Time Life Inc, 1996.

Stetoff, R., and Goetzmann, W.H., *Marco Polo and the Medieval Explorers*. Broomall, PA: Chelsea House Publishing, 1992.

Williams, B., *Ancient China*. New York: Viking Children's Books, 1996.

WEBSITES

1000 AD
www.channel4.co.uk/nextstep/1000ad

BBC Online: History
www.bbc.co.uk/history

The Black Death
www.discovery.com/stories/history/blackdeath/blackdeath.html

Byzantium 1200
www.byzantium1200.org

The Entire Bayeux Tapestry
members.tripod.com/~mr_sedivy/med_bay.html

History of Britain
www.bbc.co.uk/history/programmes/hob

History of India
www.historyofindia.com

Islam: Empire of Faith
www.pbs.org/empires/islam

The Land of Genghis Khan
www.nationalgeographic.com/features/97/genghis

Secrets of Lost Empires: A Medieval Siege
www.pbs.org/wgbh/nova/lostempires/trebuchet

The Vikings
www.pbs.org/wgbh/nova/vikings

SET INDEX